PASS THE NEW JERSEY NOTARY PUBLIC EXAM

Angelo Tropea

"Notaries Public…hold an office which can trace its origins back to ancient Rome when they were called scribae, tabellius or notarius. They are easily the oldest continuing branch of the legal profession worldwide."

ISBN: 9798387790409

Credits: page 156

The "New Jersey Notary Public Manual" (October 22, 2021) booklet by the New Jersey Department of the Treasury, Division of Revenue and Enterprise Services, can be found at :

https://www.state.nj.us/treasury/revenue/pdf/NotaryPublicManual.pdf

CONTENTS

OFFICIAL NOTARY PUBLIC WEBSITE

OFFICIAL SITE OF THE STATE OF NEW JERSEY
Department of the Treasury
Division of Revenue and Enterprise Services
Notary Public Exam

https://www.njportal.com/DOR/NotaryExam/

THE AIM OF THIS BOOK

The New Jersey Department of the Treasury, Division of Revenue and Enterprise Services, has published an excellent booklet, "New Jersey Notary Public Manual" (2021).

It contains all the law references you need to pass the New Jersey Notary Public Exam and to be a well informed and professional notary public.

The aim of this book is to complement the official publication by highlighting the more important sections of law and offering study tools to help you better prepare for the exam and become a more knowledgeable and professional practicing notary public.

THIS BOOK PROVIDES:

1. True/False, fill-in, and other "Quick Questions" to help you remember facts and definitions.

2. Multiple choice questions to help you practice for the notary public exam.

3. Practice exams to help you further solidify your knowledge of the laws relevant to notaries.

Our team believes that the combination of the above will provide the tools and the required practice to help you achieve your goal of passing the notary public exam and also increase your understanding and appreciation of laws important to notaries public.

Please Note

For simplicity, we sometimes refer to "notary public" as "notary."

"Notary Record" and "Notary Journal" are used interchangeably.

Repetition of certain concepts and questions is intentional.

If you feel that a multiple-choice question has more than one correct answer, please choose the most correct answer.

New Jersey requires that notaries public maintain one combined NOTARY JOURNAL for traditional and electronic notarial acts. We have prepared an inexpensive NOTARY JOURNAL specifically for New Jersey. It is:

"New Jersey Notary Journal Traditional and Electronic Notarial Acts."

HOW TO USE THIS BOOK

There are probably as many ways to study successfully as there are people. However, in the more than thirty years that I have been preparing study materials and conducting classes for civil service exams, I have found that certain methods seem to work better than others with the great majority of students. The following are some time-tested suggestions that you might want to consider as you incorporate this book in the study plan that is best for you.

SUGGESTIONS

1. First, read the "New Jersey Notary Public Manual" (2021) by the New Jersey Department of the Treasury, Division of Revenue and Enterprise Services. It is an excellent booklet.
It contains all the law references and facts you need to pass the New Jersey Notary Public Exam and to be a well informed and professional notary public.

2. Try the "Quick Questions" (6 on a page). Do not go on to the multiple-choice questions until you have mastered these questions. Read the comments after each answer to reinforce important facts.

3. Now tackle the multiple-choice questions (3 on page).

4. When you think you are ready, take Practice Exam 1, then Practice Exam 2, etc. Questions cover the same material but often from different angles, helping you to increase your retention of the subject matter. Also, the questions are designed to be difficult and thereby force you to "stretch" your memory to answer them. Whenever you answer a question incorrectly, review that section. Also, make sure you are confident with all the legal terms. (We have provided additional terms which will be useful to you.) They will form the basis of your understanding of the law. Study every day. Take this book with you – and make it your friend.

New Jersey statutes (Laws) are available in many places.

"New Jersey Law on Notarial Acts" is available at:

https://pub.njleg.gov/bills/2020/PL21/179_.PDF

"New applicants must attest that they have read the Manual and proceed to the testing process. The fee- based test encompasses 50 questions drawn from content in the Manual. Applicants must answer at least 80%, or 40 questions correctly, within 75 minutes, to receive a passing grade and may take the test up to three times without having to pay another test fee ($2.50). The Division permits applicants to use the Manual to answer test questions in an open book format."

- from the "Report on the Status of the State of New Jersey's Notary Education," Division of Revenue and Enterprise Services, New Jersey Department of the Treasury, September 30, 2022

FEES FOR NOTARIAL SERVICES

1. Administering oaths, taking affidavits, taking proofs of a deed, and taking acknowledgements....**$2.50 per act**.

2. Administering oaths, taking affidavits, taking proofs of a deed, and taking acknowledgments of the grantors in the transfer of real estate, regardless of the number of such services performed in a single transaction to transfer real estate....**$15.00**.

3. Administering oaths, taking affidavits, and taking acknowledgments of the mortgagors in the financing of real estate, regardless of the number of such services performed in a single transaction to finance real estate....**$25.00**.

PRACTICE QUESTIONS ON NEW JERSEY NOTARY PUBLIC MANUAL

QUESTIONS PRACTICE

In the following pages you will reinforce your understanding of the contents of the manual by answering two types of questions:

1. "Quick questions" (6 on a page) and

2. "Multiple Choice Questions" (3 on a page)

We suggest that you do not go on to the multiple-choice questions until you have mastered the Quick Questions.

When you think you are ready, take Practice Exam 1, then Practice Exam 2.

Whenever you answer a question incorrectly, review that section of law.

Also, make sure you are confident with all the legal terms.

They will form the basis of your understanding of the law.

Please note that questions in this review guide and on the actual tests may be asked in straight Question/Answer format, or the more complex "situational" question format.

We strongly believe that for learning purposes, the clarity of the "straight" Question/Answer format is more valuable.

However, some practice in answering "situational" questions may prove helpful. Because of this, the Quick Question starting with question number 109 are of the situational type.

QUICK QUESTIONS: CHAPTER 2 DEFINITIONS

1. "_____" means a declaration before a notary that the individual has signed a record, and if signed in a representative capacity, that the individual signed with proper authority.

2. "Electronic _____" is an electronic symbol, sound, or process attached or logically associated with a record and executed with intent to sign the record.

3. T/F? A person acts in a representative capacity when she is acting in her own behalf.

4. T/F? A "notarial act" applies only to tangible records (paper) and not electronic records.

5. T/F? "Notarial officer" and "Notary public" mean the exact samc thing.

6. An official stamp may be embossed on a paper record OR logically associated with an _____ record.

QUICK ANSWERS: CHAPTER 2 DEFINITIONS

1. "**Acknowledgment**" means a declaration before a notary that the individual has signed a record, and if signed in a representative capacity, that the individual signed with proper authority.

2. "Electronic **signature**" is an electronic symbol, sound, or process attached or logically associated with a record and executed with intent to sign the record.

3. **FALSE**. A person acts in a representative capacity when she acts as an authorized officer agent, partner, trustee, public officer, guardian, agent, or attorney, etc. for another person.

4. **FALSE**. A "notarial act" applies to **BOTH** tangible records (paper) and electronic records.

5. **FALSE**. A "notarial officer" may be a notary public **OR** some other person who is authorized by law to do a notarial act.

6. An official stamp may be embossed on a paper record OR logically associated with an **electronic** record.

QUICK QUESTIONS

7. A "record" may be in paper form (tangible medium) or in an _____ medium.

8. To "sign" means to execute a tangible record or attach to an electronic _____ an electronic symbol.

9. T/F? A "signature" may only be in tangible form.

10. T/F? A "stamping device" may be in physical or electronic form.

11. T/F? Verification, oath, or affirmation mean the same thing.

12. T/F? "State" means State of New Jersey, any other state and Puerto Rico.

QUICK ANSWERS

7. A "record" may be in paper form (tangible medium) or in an **electronic** medium.

8. To "sign" means to execute a tangible record or attach to an electronic **record** an electronic symbol.

9. **FALSE**. A "signature" may be in tangible form **OR** in **electronic** form.

10. **TRUE**. A "stamping device" may be in physical or electronic form.

11. **TRUE**. Verification, oath, or affirmation mean the same thing.

12. **TRUE**. "State" also means the District of Columbia, the United States Virgin Islands or territory of the United States.

QUICK QUESTIONS: CH. 3 QUALIFICATIONS, AUTHORITY, PROHIBITED ACTS

13. The minimum age to be a notary in New Jersey is _____ years old.

14. T/F? To be commissioned a notary public in New Jersey, a person must be a resident of New Jersey State.

15. T/F? A notary public may only perform notary public duties in the county where she was commissioned.

16. T/F? If a notary performs a notarial act on a record in which she has an interest, or her spouse is a party, the act is valid.

17. T/F? A notary who is not licensed as an attorney cannot advertise that he is a lawyer or attorney.

18. T/F? If a notary advertises in another language, he must include in the same advertisement a notice that he is not an attorney and does not provide immigration legal advice.

QUICK ANSWERS: CH. 3 QUALIFICATIONS, AUTHORITY, PROHIBITED ACTS

13. The minimum age to be a notary in New Jersey is **18** years old.

Notary Publics in New Jersey are commissioned for 5 years. Commissions may be renewed for additional 5-year periods.

14. **FALSE**. To be commissioned a notary public in New Jersey, a person must be a resident of New Jersey State **OR** practice (as an attorney) in New Jersey **OR** have a place of employment in New Jersey..

15. **FALSE**. A notary public may perform notary public duties throughout the State of New Jersey.

16. **FALSE**. If a notary performs a notarial act on a record in which she has an interest, or her spouse is a party, the act is **VOIDABLE**.

17. **TRUE**. A notary who is not licensed as an attorney cannot advertise that he is a lawyer or attorney.

18. **TRUE**. If a notary advertises in another language, he must include in the same advertisement a notice that he is not an attorney and does not provide immigration legal advice.

QUICK QUESTIONS: CH. 4 NOTARY COMMISSIONING PROCESS

19. An application for a notary public commission must be sent electronically to _____.

20. A renewal application or a notary public commission must be sent electronically to _____.

21. T/F? The notary public application fee is $15.

22. A non-attorney who applies to be commissioned a notary public must pass a _____ hour course.

23. A non-attorney who applies to be commissioned a notary public must pass an examination prescribed by _____.

24. What is the maximum fee that the State Treasurer can charge for each test administered online?

QUICK ANSWERS: CH. 4 NOTARY COMMISSIONING PROCESS

19. An application for a notary public commission must be sent electronically to the **State Treasurer**.

Notary Publics in New Jersey are commissioned for 5 years. Commissions may be renewed for additional 5-year periods.

20. A renewal application for a notary public commission must be sent electronically to the **State Treasurer.**

Notary Publics in New Jersey are commissioned for 5 years. Commissions may be renewed for additional 5- year periods.

21. **FALSE.** The notary public application fee is **$25**.

22. A non-attorney who applies to be commissioned a notary public must pass a **6 (SIX)** hour course.

23. A non-attorney who applies to be commissioned a notary public must pass an examination prescribed by **the State Treasurer**.

24. The maximum fee that the State Treasurer can charge for each test administered online is **$15**.

QUICK QUESTIONS

25. The _____ provides completion certificates of required education and testing.

26. A _resident_ notary shall take an oath within 3 months of receipt of original or renewal commission before which public officer?

27. A _nonresident_ notary shall take an oath within 3 months of receipt of original or renewal commission before which public officer?

28. The certificate of commission and qualification of a notary must be transmitted by the clerk of county to the State Treasurer within ___ days of the administration of the oath.

29. T/F? The State Treasurer must cancel and revoke a notary commission if oath is not taken within 30 days of receipt of the commission.

30. A notary who changes her name from the one she was commissioned shall notify the _____ and specify the circumstances of the name change.

QUICK ANSWERS

25. The **State Treasurer** provides completion certificates of required education and testing.

26. A resident notary shall take an oath before **the clerk of county in which he resides** within 3 months of receipt of original or renewal commission.

27. A nonresident notary shall take an oath within 3 months of receipt of original or renewal commission before **the clerk of county where the notary has a place of business or where he is employed.**

28. The certificate of commission and qualification of a notary must be transmitted by the clerk of county to the State Treasurer within **10 days** of the administration of the oath.

29. **FALSE.** The State Treasurer must cancel and revoke a notary commission if oath is not taken within **3 MONTHS** of receipt of the commission.

Also, such commission is null and void.

30. A notary who changes her name from the one she was commissioned shall notify the **State Treasurer** and specify the circumstances of the name change.

QUICK QUESTIONS: CH. 5 COMMISSION DENIAL, REVOCATION, SUSPENSION....

31. The _____ may deny a notary public commission if the applicant committed an incompetent or dishonest act which demonstrates that the applicant does not have the competence or reliability necessary to be a notary public.

32. T/F? A person may be denied a notary public commission due to conviction of any crime.

33. T/F? A person may be denied a notary public recommission due to failure to discharge any duty required by law.

34. If the State Treasurer is going to deny an application for a notary public commission, it must send a notice to _____.

35. If an applicant waives his right to appeal a decision of the State Treasurer regarding an application for a notary commission, the decision of the Treasurer becomes a _____.

36. An appeal of a decision regarding a notary commission goes to the _____ _____ of the Superior Court.

QUICK ANSWERS: CH. 5 COMMISSION DENIAL. REVOCATION, SUSPENSION....

31. The **State Treasurer** may deny a notary public commission if the applicant committed an incompetent or dishonest act which demonstrates that the applicant does not have the competence or reliability necessary to be a notary public.

32. **FALSE.** A person may be denied a notary public commission due to conviction of a crime of the **SECOND DEGREE OR ABOVE**.

33. **TRUE.** A person may be denied a notary public recommission due to failure to discharge any duty required by law. Also, may be denied a commission for false or misleading advertising, giving legal advice, acting as a consultant in immigration matters, denial of application for notary in another state, etc.

34. If the State Treasurer is going to deny an application for a notary public commission, it must send a notice to **the applicant.**

35. If an applicant waives his right to appeal a decision of the State Treasurer regarding an application for a notary commission, the decision of the Treasurer becomes a **final decision**.

36. An appeal of a decision regarding a notary commission goes to the **Appellate Division** of the Superior Court.

QUICK QUESTIONS: CHAPTER 6 GENERAL REQUIREMENTS OF NOTARIAL ACTS

37. Notarial acts are evidenced by a _____ and stamp by the notary public.

38. T/F? Notarial certificates may be executed days after the performance of the notarial act.

39. Who signs and dates the notarial certificate?

40. T/F? A notarial certificate does not have to state the jurisdiction where the notarial act is performed.

41. A notarial certificate has the title of the _____ of the notarial officer.

42. T/F? A notarial certificate by a notary public must state the commencement date of the notarial officer's commission.

QUICK ANSWERS: CHAPTER 6 GENERAL REQUIREMENTS OF NOTARIAL ACTS

37. Notarial acts are evidenced by a **CERTIFICATE** and stamp by the notary public.

38. **FALSE.** Notarial certificates must be executed **at the same time** (contemporaneously) as the notarial act.

39. The **notarial officer** signs and dates the notarial certificate.

40. **FALSE.** A notarial certificate **must** state the jurisdiction where the notarial act is performed.

41. A notarial certificate has the title of the **office** of the notarial officer.

42. **FALSE.** A notarial certificate by a notary public must state the **EXPIRATION** date of the notarial officer's commission.

QUICK QUESTIONS

43. When is the signature of the notary affixed or logically associated with (in the case of an electronic notary) to a document?

44. In the case of a paper record, the notarial certificate (MAY? / MUST?) be attached to the record.

45. The notary public official stamp must include the name of _____.

46. T/F? The notary public official stamp must include the notary public's commission commencement date.

47. In what location on the document page must the official stamp be affixed?

48. Who is responsible for keeping a notary stamp secure?

QUICK ANSWERS

43. The signature of the notary is affixed or logically associated with (in the case of an electronic notary) to a document **AFTER** the notarial act has been performed.

44. In the case of a paper record, the notarial certificate **MUST** be attached to the record.

45. The notary public official stamp must include the name of **the notary**.

46. **FALSE**. The notary public official stamp must include the notary public's commission **EXPIRATION** date.

47. The official stamp must be affixed **near the signature of the notary public**.

48. The **notary public** is responsible for keeping a notary stamp secure.

QUICK QUESTIONS

49. A notary public cannot allow another person to use his stamp, except for which instance?

50. T/F? If an employer pays for a notary public device, then the device is the property of the employer.

51. T/F? If a notary stamping device is stolen, the notary must inform the State Treasurer within 30 calendar days.

52. A notary public (MAY? / MUST?) maintain a notary journal.

53. T/F? A notary public journal must be maintained in a tangible medium.

54. Must a notary maintain separate journals for tangible and electronic notarizations?

QUICK ANSWERS

49. A notary public cannot allow another person to use his stamp, <u>**except when the notary cannot physically use the device.**</u>

50. **FALSE**. If an employer pays for a notary public device, the device is <u>**NOT**</u> the property of the employer. It is the property of the notary public.

51. **FALSE**. If a notary stamping device is stolen, the notary must inform the State Treasurer within <u>**10 (TEN)**</u> calendar days.

52. A notary public <u>**MUST**</u> maintain a notary journal.

53. **FALSE**. A notary public journal may be maintained in a tangible medium <u>**OR IN AN ELECTRONIC FORMAT.**</u>

54. **NO**. A notary must maintain <u>**ONE**</u> JOURNAL at a time to record both tangible and electronic notarial acts.

QUICK QUESTIONS

55. T/F? A journal maintained on a tangible medium, must be a permanent, bound register.

56. If a notary journal is maintained in an electronic format, it must be in a permanent and _____ evident format.

57. T/F? The notary journal must contain the date and time of the notarial act, and the type of notarial act.

58. T/F? The notary journal must contain <u>the name and age of each person for whom a notarial act was performed.</u>

59. If the notary knows an individual because of personal knowledge, what must the notary record in the journal?

60. If the notary identified an individual by an identity document (ID) the notary must record in the journal the date of issuance and _____ of the identity document.

QUICK ANSWERS

55.
TRUE. A journal maintained on a tangible medium, must be a permanent, bound register.

Also, must have consecutively numbered lines and consecutively numbered pages.

56. If a notary journal is maintained in an electronic format, it must be in a permanent and **TAMPER-evident** format.

57. **TRUE**. The notary journal must contain the date and time of the notarial act, and the type of notarial act.

58. **FALSE**. The notary journal must contain the name and **ADDRESS** of each person for whom a notarial act was performed.

59. If the notary knows an individual because of personal knowledge, the notary must record in the journal a statement to that effect.

60. If the notary identified an individual by an identity document (ID) the notary must record in the journal the date of issuance and **expiration** of the identity document.

QUICK QUESTIONS

61. T/F? A notary must record in the notarial journal an itemized list of fees charged for the notarial act only if the fees total exceeds $20.00.

62. If the notary journal is stolen or lost, the notary must notify the State Treasurer within _____ days (at the State Treasurer's online site).

63. T?F? A notary must retain her journal for 3 years after the notarial act.

64. If a notary dies or becomes incompetent, the representative must contact the State Treasurer within _____ days for instructions on how to submit the notary journal to the State Treasurer.

65. T/F? An attorney who is a notary may instead of maintaining a notary journal maintain a record of notarial acts in his office files.

66. T/F? The fees charged for a notarial act may be recorded in a notary journal as one sum amount.

QUICK ANSWERS

61. **FALSE.** A notary MUST record in the notarial journal an <u>itemized list</u> of fees charged for the notarial act (regardless of the total amount charged).

62. If the notary journal is stolen or lost, the notary must notify the State Treasurer within **10 (TEN) days** (at the State Treasurer's online site).

63. **FALSE**. A notary must retain her journal for **10 (TEN) years** after the notarial act. (or contact the State Treasurer for instructions on how to submit the notary journal to the State Treasurer).

64. If a notary dies or becomes incompetent, the representative must contact the State Treasurer within **45 days** for instructions on how to submit the notary journal to the State Treasurer.

65. **TRUE.** An attorney who is a notary may instead of maintaining a notary journal maintain a record of notarial acts in his office files.

66. **FALSE.** The fees charged for a notarial act must be itemized.

CHAPTER 7 QUICK QUESTIONS: FORMS OF ID AND COPY CERTIFICATION

67. A notarial officer who _____ a copy of a record must determine that the copy is a full, true, and accurate reproduction of the record.

68. A notary may satisfy herself as to the identity of an individual by satisfactory evidence or by _____.

69. T/F? Valid forms of satisfactory evidence of identity include a passport, driver's license, or government-issued, non-driver ID card.

70. A valid form of government-issued ID is ID which is current or not expired more than 3 years and contains the person's signature or photograph of the _____ (part of body) of the person.

71. For and ID to be accepted as proof of identity, the ID presented to the notarial officer must be _____ to the notarial officer.

72. T/F? A notarial officer may require additional ID credentials to be assured of the identity of the person.

CHAPTER 7 QUICK ANSWERS: FORMS OF ID AND COPY CERTIFICATION

67. A notarial officer who **certifies** a copy of a record must determine that the copy is a full, true, and accurate reproduction of the record.

68. A notary may satisfy herself as to the identity of an individual by satisfactory evidence or by **personal knowledge**.

69. **TRUE**. Valid forms of satisfactory evidence of identity include a passport, driver's license, or government-issued, non- driver ID card.

(The non-driver ID must be current or expired not more than 3 years before the notarial act is performed.)

70. A valid form of government-issued ID is ID which is current or not expired more than 3 years and contains the person's signature or photograph of the **face** of the person.

71. For and ID to be accepted as proof of identity, the ID presented to the notarial officer must be **satisfactory** to the notarial officer.

72. **TRUE**. A notarial officer may require additional ID credentials to be assured of the identity of the person.

CHAPTER 8 QUICK QUESTIONS: USE OF COMMUNICATION TECHNOLOGY

73. T/F? For every notarial act, the person (principal) must personally appear before the notary.

74. A systems that uses fingerprints, facial, and voice patterns to identify a person is referred to as a _____ identification system.

75. Communication technology allows a notarial officer to communicate to a remotely located individual and also to communicate with persons who have vision, hearing, and speech _____.

76. An electronic _____ issued to a party to electronically identify a person is called a "Digital Public key certificate."

77. A political entity (other than a U.S. state, an Indian tribe, or the United States) is known as a _____ state.

78. Identity _____ involves using information from private or public sources to identify a person.

CHAPTER 8 QUICK ANSWERS: USE OF COMMUNICATION TECHNOLOGY

73. **FALSE**. For every notarial act, the person (principal) must personally appear before the notary **or shall use communication technology to appear before the notarial officer.**

74. A systems that uses fingerprints, facial, and voice patterns to identify a person is referred to as a **biometric** identification system.

75. Communication technology allows a notarial officer to communicate to a remotely located individual and also to communicate with persons who have vision, hearing, and speech **impairment** (disability).

76. An electronic **credential** issued to a party to electronically identify a person is called a "Digital Public key certificate."

77. A political entity (other than a U.S. state, an Indian tribe, or the United States) is known as a "**foreign**" state.

78. Identity **proofing** involves using information from private or public sources to identify a person.

QUICK QUESTIONS

79. If a person is not in the physical presence of a notary, that person is said to be _____ located.

80. A notary who intends on doing remote notarization must notify the State _____ before doing any remote notarization.

81. A notarial act that is done using remote technology for a person that is located in a remote location is considered done in New Jersey and is governed by _____ law.

82. T/F? For remote notarization, the person for whom the notarial act is performed must be located within the state of New Jersey.

83. T/F? Security features for a remote session are governed by the rules of the National Association of Certified Public Accountants.

84. Methods of electronic proofing include Dynamic Knowledge-Based Authentication, Biometric Identity Verification, and Digital _____ ___ _____.

QUICK ANSWERS

79. If a person is not in the physical presence of a notary, that person is said to be **remotely** located.

80. A notary who intends on doing remote notarization must notify the State **Treasurer** before doing any remote notarization.

81. A notarial act that is done using remote technology for a person that is located in a remote location is considered done in New Jersey and is governed by **New Jersey** law.

82. **FALSE**. For remote notarization, the person for whom the notarial act is performed does **NOT** have to be located within the state of New Jersey.

83. **FALSE**. Security features for a remote session are governed by the rules of the **National Notary Association**.

84. Methods of electronic proofing include Dynamic Knowledge-Based Authentication, Biometric Identity Verification, and Digital **Public Key Certificate**.

QUICK QUESTIONS

85. For remote notarization for an individual outside the United States, the notarial act must be for property located in the U.S. or for a transaction that is substantially connected to _____.

86. T/F? A notary public shall not perform a notarial act for a tangible record not physically in the presence of the notary.

87. T/F? The date of effectiveness of a notarial act is the date that the declaration (attached to the remote notarial act) was signed by the individual that was located remotely.

88. T/F? The audio-visual record of an individual taking an oath must be retained by the remote notary for 3 years.

89. Retention of Audio-Visual recordings for a deceased notarial officer is for a period of _____ years.

90. If a guardian is appointed for a notarial officer, for how many years must the guardian retain the audio-visual records of the notarial officer?

QUICK ANSWERS

85. For remote notarization for an individual outside the United States, the notarial act must be for property located in the U.S. or for a transaction that is substantially connected to **the United States.**

86. **FALSE**. A notary public **MAY** perform a notarial act for a tangible record not physically in the presence of the notary.

87. **TRUE**. The date of effectiveness of a notarial act is the date that the declaration (attached to the remote notarial act) was signed by the individual that was located remotely.

88. **FALSE**. The audio-visual record of an individual taking an oath must be retained by the remote notary for **10 (TEN)** years.

89. Retention of Audio-Visual recordings for a deceased notarial officer is for a period of **10 (TEN)** years.

90. If a guardian is appointed for a notarial officer, the guardian must retain the audio-visual records of the notarial officer for **10 (TEN) years**.

CHAPTER 9 QUICK QUESTIONS: ELECTRONIC NOTARIZATION

91. Who selects which tamper-evident technology to use for electronic notarization?

92. "Tamper-evident" technology is technology that records evidence of any _____ made in a record.

93. T/F? After executing the notarial act, a notary who executes an electronic notarial act must complete an electronic certificate with an electronic signature and stamp and attach the certificate, signature, and stamp to (or logically associate the certificate and stamp) with the notarized record.

94. T/F? To be considered reliable, an electronic signature and stamp must be generic.

95. T/F? To be considered reliable, an electronic signature and stamp must be capable of independent verification.

96. T/F? Generally, the notary must not disclose any information which allows access to electronic affixing methods used.

CHAPTER 9 QUICK ANSWERS: ELECTRONIC NOTARIZATION

91. The **notarial officer** selects which tamper-evident technology to use for electronic notarization.

92. "Tamper-evident" technology is technology that records evidence of any **change** made in a record.

93. **TRUE**. After executing the notarial act, a notary who executes an electronic notarial act must complete an electronic certificate with an electronic signature and stamp and attach the certificate, signature, and stamp to (or logically associate the certificate and stamp) with the notarized record.

94. **FALSE**. To be considered reliable, an electronic signature and stamp must be **unique to the notarial officer**.

95. **TRUE**. To be considered reliable, an electronic signature and stamp must be capable of independent verification.

Must also be under the notary's constant control and must be logically associated with the document in a tamper-evident format.

96. **TRUE**. Generally, the notary must not disclose any information which allows access to electronic affixing methods used. (EXCEPT when requested by law enforcement or legal process.)

QUICK QUESTIONS

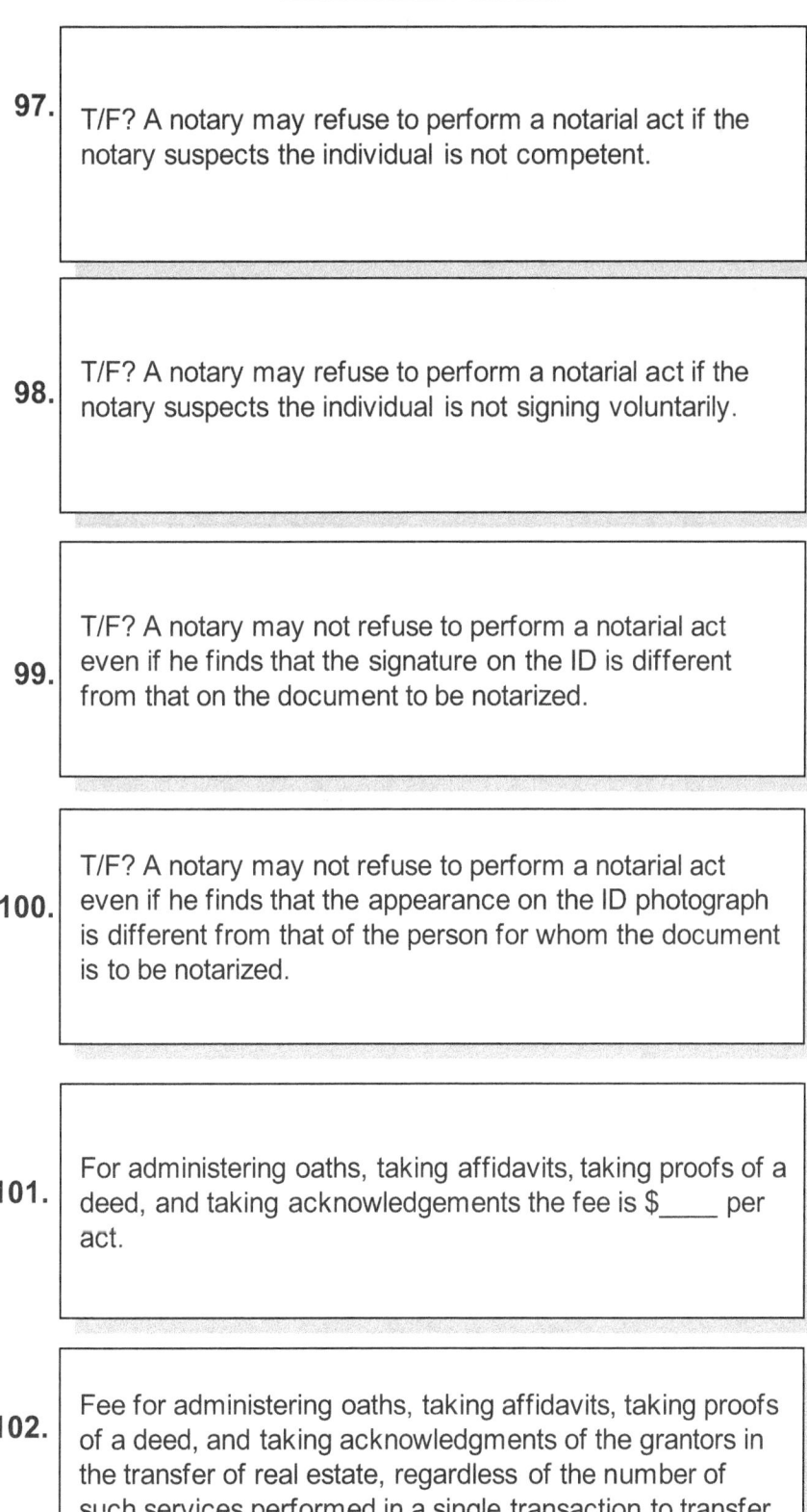

97. T/F? A notary may refuse to perform a notarial act if the notary suspects the individual is not competent.

98. T/F? A notary may refuse to perform a notarial act if the notary suspects the individual is not signing voluntarily.

99. T/F? A notary may not refuse to perform a notarial act even if he finds that the signature on the ID is different from that on the document to be notarized.

100. T/F? A notary may not refuse to perform a notarial act even if he finds that the appearance on the ID photograph is different from that of the person for whom the document is to be notarized.

101. For administering oaths, taking affidavits, taking proofs of a deed, and taking acknowledgements the fee is $____ per act.

102. Fee for administering oaths, taking affidavits, taking proofs of a deed, and taking acknowledgments of the grantors in the transfer of real estate, regardless of the number of such services performed in a single transaction to transfer real estate is $_____.

QUICK ANSWERS

97. **TRUE** A notary may refuse to perform a notarial act if the notary suspects the individual is not competent.

98. **TRUE**. A notary may refuse to perform a notarial act if the notary suspects the individual is not signing voluntarily.

99. **FALSE**. A notary **MAY** refuse to perform a notarial act even if he finds that the signature on the ID is different from that on the document to be notarized

100. **FALSE**. A notary **MAY** refuse to perform a notarial act if he finds that the appearance on the ID photograph is different from that of the person for whom the document is to be notarized.

101. For administering oaths, taking affidavits, taking proofs of a deed, and taking acknowledgements the fee is **$2.50** per act.

102. Fee for administering oaths, taking affidavits, taking proofs of a deed, and taking acknowledgments of the grantors in the transfer of real estate, regardless of the number of such services performed in a single transaction to transfer real estate is **$15.00**.

QUICK QUESTIONS

103. Fee for administering oaths, taking affidavits, and taking acknowledgments of the mortgagors in the financing of real estate, regardless of the number of such services performed in a single transaction to finance real estate is $_____.

104. T/F? The notarial fee for administering an oath to two persons individually is $2.50 total.

105. T/F? The notarial fee for taking an affidavit and for taking an acknowledgement is the same.

106. T/F? The fee for administering oaths, taking affidavits, and taking acknowledgments of the mortgagors in the financing of real estate depends upon the number of notarial acts performed.

107. The fee for administering oaths, taking affidavits, and taking acknowledgments of the mortgagors in the _____ of real estate, regardless of the number of such services performed in a single transaction to finance real estate is $25.00.

108. If a notary performs both traditional (tangible) notarization and electronic notarization, how many notary journals must the notary maintain at any one time?

QUICK ANSWERS

103. Fee for administering oaths, taking affidavits, and taking acknowledgments of the mortgagors in the financing of real estate, regardless of the number of such services performed in a single transaction to finance real estate is **$25.00**.

104. **FALSE.** The notarial fee for administering an oath to **two** persons individually is **$5.00** ($2.50 for each notarial act of administering an oath.).

105. **TRUE.** The notarial fee for taking an affidavit and for taking an acknowledgement is the same. **($2.50 per act)**.

106. **FALSE.** The fee for administering oaths, taking affidavits, and taking acknowledgments of the mortgagors in the financing of real estate **regardless of the number of such services performed in a single transaction to transfer real estate is $15.00**.

107. The fee for administering oaths, taking affidavits, and taking acknowledgments of the mortgagors in the **financing** of real estate, regardless of the number of such services performed in a single transaction to finance real estate is $25.00.

108. If a notary performs both traditional (tangible) notarization and electronic notarization, the notary must maintain **ONLY ONE NOTARY JOURNAL AT ANY ONE TIME.**

CHAPTER 10: SITUATIONAL-TYPE QUICK QUESTIONS

109. James Faulkner makes a declaration before a notary that he did indeed sign the record presented to the notary. This declaration is called __ _____.

110. Susan Williams does not want to "swear an oath." The notary informs her that she can instead "_____" as to the truthfulness of her statements.

111. Barbara Johnson is 17 years old and has just started working as a secretary in a real estate office. She tells her employer that she would like to be commissioned a notary and asks what is the minimum age required to be commissioned a notary. How should the employer respond?

112. Notary public David Atwell receives a phone call from a resident of a county in New Jersey that is different from the county in which he was commissioned a notary. The man needs a document notarized and asks if Mr. Atwell is empowered to act in his county. How should Mr. Atwell respond?

113. The wife of Lawrence Thomson, a notary commissioned in New Jersey, asks if he can please notarize her signature on a government job application. How should Mr. Thomson respond?

114. Barbara James works in a real estate office part time while she attends her second year of law school. She is a commissioned notary public and would like to advertise in the window that she provides notarial services and that she is an attorney. What should her employer tell Ms. James?

CHAPTER 10: SITUATIONAL-TYPE QUICK ANSWERS

109. James Faulkner makes a declaration before a notary that he did indeed sign the record presented to the notary. This declaration is called **an acknowledgment**.

110. Susan Williams does not want to "swear an oath." The notary informs her that she can instead "**AFFIRM**" as to the truthfulness of her statements.

111. The employer should inform Ms. Johnson that the minimum age to be commissioned a notary public is **18**.

112. Mr. Atwell should inform the caller that he is empowered to act as a notary in any county in the State of New Jersey.

113. Mr. Thomson should inform his wife that he cannot notarize her signature because a notary is prohibited from performing a notarial act on any record in which he or his spouse has an interest.

114. The employer should inform Ms. James that she is not yet an attorney and therefore cannot advertise that she provides attorney services.

QUICK QUESTIONS

115. The employer of Harry Lawson wishes to pay the notary public application fee for him. The employer believes it is $35 and hands him $35. What should Harry Lawson tell his employer?

116. Elaine Madison receives her original commission on June 10. She has to take an oath of office within how many months of the receipt of the commission?

117. Benjamin Davidson, a commissioned notary public, changed his name legally to Ben David. Which government official must he notify of his name change?

118. Conner Thiel was convicted of a crime in the second degree. He wants to be commissioned a notary public. He asks his notary friend if he qualifies to be a notary. How should his friend respond?

119. Conner Thiel applies to be a notary public. However, the State Treasurer denies the application based on Mr. Thiel's criminal record. Mr. Thiel wishes to appeal and asks his friend to which court he should appeal. How should his friend respond?

120. At a house closing, the notary signs the paper on page eight and by mistake the attorney hands the notary page seven to affix the official stamp. What should the notary tell the attorney?

QUICK ANSWERS

115. Harry Lawson should inform his employer that the notary public application fee is only **$25**.

116. Ms. Madison must take an oath of office within **3 MONTHS** of the receipt of the commission.

117. Ben David must notify the **State Treasurer** and specify the circumstances of the name change.

118. Conner Thiel's friend should inform him that a person may be denied a notary public commission due to conviction of a **crime** of the **SECOND DEGREE OR ABOVE.**

119. The friend of Connor Thiel should inform him that appeals regarding a notary commission go to the **Appellate Term of the Superior Court**.

120. The notary should tell the attorney to hand him page eight because the official stamp must be affixed **near the signature of the notary public.**

QUICK QUESTIONS

121. Kim Fox is a newly commissioned notary and works at a real estate company. Her employer suggests that she leave her notary stamp with him nights and weekends and that he will secure the notary stamp in his office safe. What should she respond to her employer?

122. On a busy day in the real estate office where she works, Jane Ecker, a notary public, is asked by her coworker to share her stamp because the coworker cannot locate her stamp. What should Ms. Ecker tell her coworker?

123. Maria Velez is a notary public. One day after shopping, she notices that her car door was broken into and that her notary stamp is missing. She knows that she must report the stolen stamp to the State Treasurer. How many days does she have to do so?

124. Bernard Binkins moved to New Jersey from a state where he was commissioned a notary public but did not have to maintain a journal. He is planning to become a New Jersey notary and asked his coworker if he would have to maintain one in New Jersey. How should his coworker respond?

125. Bob Garner will soon be a commissioned notary public in New Jersey. He is required to maintain a notary journal. In what medium must the journal be?

126. Pat Lane is shopping online for a notary journal. She notices that some journals are in looseleaf form and that other journals are in bound, permanent form. Which journal type should she purchase?

QUICK ANSWERS

121. She should inform her employer that the **notary public** is responsible for keeping a notary stamp secure.

122. Ms. Ecker should tell her coworker that a notary public cannot allow another person to use her stamp, **except when the notary cannot physically use the device (for example, an injury or physical disability of the notary)**.

123. Ms. Velez has **10 calendar days** to report the theft to the State Treasurer.

124. The coworker should inform Mr. Binkins that a person commissioned a notary public in New Jersey is required to maintain a notary journal.

125. A notary public journal may be maintained in a tangible medium (such as a bound book format) **OR IN AN ELECTRONIC FORMAT**.

126. In New Jersey, a journal maintained on a tangible medium (book format), must be a permanent, bound register.

QUICK QUESTIONS

127. Frank Benson is performing a notarial act for an individual whom he knows by personal knowledge. What must Frank Benson record in his notary journal?

128. Eleanor Jones, a notary public, identifies an individual by using an identity document. What dates from the identity document must she record in her notary journal?

129. Ed Harris performs notarial acts totaling $7.50 during a session ($2.50, $2.50, and $2.50). What specific amount(s) must he record in the notary journal?

130. George Marks just filled up a notary journal book and stores it in his office. How long must George Marks retain the notary journal?

131. Larry Collins, a 92 years old notary is declared incompetent by the court. How long does his representative have to contact the State Treasurer for instructions on how to submit the notary journal to the State Treasurer?

132. Kyle Asher asks Bryan Vargas, a notary what type of government issued ID is satisfactory ID. How should Mr. Vargas respond to the question?

QUICK ANSWERS

127. Frank Benson must record in his notarial journal a statement to the effect that he knows the person by personal knowledge.

128. Eleanor Jones must record in the notary journal the date of issuance and the date of expiration of the identity document.

129. Ed Harris MUST record in the notarial journal an itemized list of fees charged for the notarial act (regardless of the total amount charged). Therefore, he should record $2.50, $2.50, and $2.50, and specify the notarial act for each fee collected.

130. George Marks must retain the notary journal book for **10 (TEN) years** after the notarial act.

131. The representative must contact the State Treasurer within **45 days** of the declaration of incompetency for instructions on how to submit the notary journal to the State Treasurer.

132. Mr. Vargas should respond by saying that a valid form of government-issued ID is ID which is current or not expired more than 3 years and contains the signature or photograph of the face of the person.

QUICK QUESTIONS

133. Jim Samuels has a broken leg which is in a cast and asks a notary if the notary could perform a notarial act without Mr. Samuels physically appearing in front of the notary. How should the notary respond?

134. Chris Holmes, a notary, asks another notary, his coworker, where he may find examples of certificate forms. How should the coworker answer?

135. Pamela Jenkins is a notary public who wishes to do remote notarization. Which official must she inform of her intention to do remote notarization?

136. Arvin Cronin is a notary who performs remote notarization. He is contacted by a person living in California who asks if Mr. Cronin can do a notarization even if the person is not physically in New Jersey. How should Mr. Cronin respond?

137. Alan Shaw performs a remote notarization for which he made an audio-visual recording of the person taking an oath. For how many years must Mr. Shaw retain the audio-visual recording?

138. Elma Green, a notary, is asked by Lorna Davidson (age 96) to take her acknowledgment. Ms. Green suspects that Ms. Davidson is not mentally competent. What options does Ms. Green have with respect to performing the notarial act?

QUICK ANSWERS

133. The notary should respond by saying that for every notarial act, the person (principal) must personally appear before the notary **OR shall use communication technology to appear before the notarial officer.**

134. The coworker should answer by saying that forms of certificates may be found in the official publication, "New Jersey Notary Public Manual."

135. A notary who intends on doing remote notarization must notify the **State Treasurer** before doing any remote notarization.

136. He should respond that if the notary act is otherwise authorized, the mere fact that the person is not physically in New Jersey is not a bar to the notary performing remote notarization.

137. The audio-visual record of an individual taking an oath must be retained by the notary for **10 (TEN)** years.

138. Ms. Green may refuse to perform a notarial act if the notary suspects the individual is not competent.

QUICK QUESTIONS

139. Charles Dell asks Paul Jenker, a notary public, what is the fee for taking an affidavit and for taking an acknowledgment. How should Mr. Jenker respond?

140. If a person does not want to "swear an oath," the person may instead "_____" as to the truthfulness of the statement.

141. A software developer offers a remote technology to a notary to perform notarial acts. He states that it has been used in other states. The New Jersey notary asks if the technology is "tamper-evident." The developer answers "No." Can the notary use the technology?

142. Diane Hunter works as a secretary in a real estate office where she also performs notarial acts. One evening, Diane forgets to secure her notarial stamp before leaving. She remembers when she is outside the building. What is the proper action for Diane to take?

143. Arlene Keller is a notary public who performs remote notarization. One day her computer fails to load the program. Her friend tells her she can help, but that she needs information regarding the electronic affixing methods used by the program. How should Ms. Keller respond?

144. Ken Williams works in a real estate office and also is a notary. A new employee wishes to send her application for a notary commission to the State Treasurer and asks Mr. Williams if he knows the address where she should mail it. How should Ken Williams respond?

QUICK ANSWERS

139. He should respond by saying that the notarial fee for taking an affidavit and for taking an acknowledgement is the same. ($2.50 per act).

140. If a person does not want to "swear an oath," the person may instead "**affirm**" as to the truthfulness of the statement

141. The New Jersey notary **cannot** use the technology because one of the requirements of remote technology in New Jersey is that it be "**tamper-evident**."

142. Diane should return to the office and secure her stamp because notaries public are responsible for securing their stamps.

143. Ms. Keller should inform her friend that a notary must not disclose any information which allows access to electronic affixing methods used.

144. He should inform the employee that an application for a notary public commission must be sent **electronically** to the State Treasurer.

MULTIPLE CHOICE QUESTIONS

1. "_____" means a declaration before a notary that the individual has signed a record, and if signed in a representative capacity, that the individual signed with proper authority.

   A. affidavit

   B. contract

   C. compliance

   D. acknowledgment

2. Choose the best answer. A document may be:

   A. physical (tangible)

   B. electronic

   C. physical (tangible) or electronic

   D. None of the above choices are correct.

3. "In a representative capacity" means acting as:

   A. the partner of a person.

   B. a shareholder of a corporation.

   C. an authorized representative of another in a capacity

   D. none of the above

MULTIPLE CHOICE ANSWERS

1.

D. acknowledgment

"**Acknowledgment**" means a declaration before a notary that the individual has signed a record, and if signed in a representative capacity, that the individual signed with proper authority.

2.

C. physical (tangible) or electronic.

A document may be physical (tangible) or electronic.

3.

C. an authorized representative of another in a capacity

"In a representative capacity" means acting as an authorized representative of another in a capacity.

MULTIPLE CHOICE QUESTIONS

4.

Which of the following is NOT included in the meaning of a "notarial act?"

A. taking a verification.

B. acting as an executor.

C. witnessing a signature.

D. administering an oath.

5.

Who commissions a notary public?

A. the Governor

B. the mayor of cities with a population over 100,000

C. the State Treasurer

D. none of the above

6.

Choose the best answer. To "sign" means:

A. to execute a tangible record

B. to associate with an electronic record an electronic

symbol

C. Both A and B.

D. neither A nor B

MULTIPLE CHOICE ANSWERS

4.

B. acting as an executor

Acting as an "executor" is **NOT** included in the meaning of "notarial act." An executor is a person appointed in a will to handle the estate of a deceased person.

5.

C. the State Treasurer

The officer who commissions notaries in New Jersey is the State Treasurer.

6.

C. Both A and B.

To "sign" means to execute a tangible record, and to associate with an electronic record an electronic symbol.

CH. 3: QUALIFICATIONS, AUTHORITY, PROHIBITED ACTS

MULTIPLE CHOICE QUESTIONS

7.

The minimum age to be a notary public in New Jersey is:

A. 16

B. 18

C. 21

D. 25

8.

Which of the following choices is most correct? To be commissioned a notary public in New Jersey, a person may be the following:

A. a resident of New Jersey

B. employed in New Jersey

C. an attorney practicing in New Jersey

D. All of the above are correct.

9.

A notary public commissioned in New Jersey may perform his duties:

A. only in his state of birth.

B. only in the county where he is commissioned.

C. only in the county of commission and adjoining counties.

D. throughout the State of New Jersey.

CH. 3: QUALIFICATIONS, AUTHORITY, PROHIBITED ACTS
MULTIPLE CHOICE ANSWERS

7.
B. 18

The minimum age to be a notary public in New Jersey is **18**.

8.
D. All of the above are correct.

To be commissioned a notary in New Jersey, a person may be **1) a resident of New Jersey, OR 2) employed in New Jersey, OR 3) an attorney practicing in New Jersey**.

9.
D. throughout the State of New Jersey.

A notary public commissioned in New Jersey may perform his duties **throughout the State of New Jersey**.

MULTIPLE CHOICE QUESTIONS

10.

Which of the following notarial acts are voidable?

1) a notarial act where the notary has a direct interest

2) a notarial act where the spouse of the notary is a party

A. number 1 only

B. number 2 only

C. both 1 and 2

D. neither 1 nor 2

11.

If a notary advertises in another language, he must include in the same advertisement a notice that:

1) he is not an attorney

2) he does not provide immigration legal advice.

A. 1 only

B. 2 only

C. both 1 and 2

D. neither 1 nor 2

12.

A notary may advertise that he is an attorney:

A. if he is a college graduate.

B. if he has had some legal experience.

C. If he has worked as a legal assistant.

D. none of the above.

MULTIPLE CHOICE ANSWERS

10.

<u>C</u>. **both 1 and 2**

A notarial act where the notary has a direct interest **AND** a notarial act where the spouse of the notary is a party are **BOTH VOIDABLE**.

11.

<u>C</u>. **both 1 and 2**

If a notary advertises in another language, he must include in the same advertisement a notice that:

1) he is not an attorney **AND**

2) he does not provide immigration legal advice.

12.

D. none of the above.

A notary who is a non-attorney is prohibited from advertising that he is an attorney or that he renders any legal services.

QUICK QUESTIONS CH. 4: NOTARY COMMISSIONING PROCESS

13. An application or a renewal application for a notary public commission must be sent electronically to which of the following?

A. the Secretary of State

B. the County Clerk

C. the Office of the Governor

D. the State Treasurer

14. The fee for the notary public application is which of the following amounts?

A. $15

B. $20

C. $25

D. none of the above

15. What is the maximum fee that the State Treasurer can charge for each test administered online?

A. $15

B. $20

C. $25

D. none of the above

QUICK ANSWERS CH. 4: NOTARY COMMISSIONING PROCESS

13.

D. the State Treasurer

An application or a renewal application for a notary public commission must be sent electronically to **the State Treasurer**.

Notary Publics in New Jersey are commissioned for 5 years. Commissions may be renewed for additional 5-year periods.

14.

C. $25

The notary public application fee is **$25.**

15.

A. $15

The maximum fee that the State Treasurer can charge for each test administered online is **$15**.

MULTIPLE CHOICE QUESTIONS

16.

A resident or nonresident notary shall take an oath within 3 months of receipt of original or renewal commission before which public officer?

A. County Clerk

B. State Controller

C. State Treasurer

D. none of the above

17.

The State Treasurer must cancel and revoke a notary commission if the oath is not taken within _____ of receipt of the commission.

A. 30 days

B. two months

C. 3 months

D. none of the above

18.

A notary who changes her name from the one she was commissioned shall notify the _____ and specify the circumstances of the name change.

A. County Clerk

B. State Controller

C. State Treasurer

D. none of the above

MULTIPLE CHOICE ANSWERS

16.

A. County Clerk

A resident or nonresident notary shall take an oath within 3 months of receipt of original or renewal commission before the **county clerk** in the county where he works or has a place of business, if he is not a resident of New Jersey.

17.

C. 3 months

The State Treasurer must cancel and revoke a notary commission if the oath is not taken within **3 months** of receipt of the commission.

18.

C. State Treasurer

A notary who changes her name from the one she was commissioned shall notify the **State Treasurer** and specify the circumstances of the name change.

MULTIPLE CHOICE QUES. CH. 5: COMMISSION DENIAL. REVOCATION, SUSPENSION...

19. The _____ may deny a notary public commission if the applicant committed an incompetent or dishonest act which demonstrates that the applicant does not have the competence or reliability necessary to be a notary public.

A. Governor

B. State Controller

C. State Treasurer

D. County Clerk

20. Which of the following two choices are correct? A person may be denied a notary public commission due to:

1) conviction of a crime of the second degree or above

2) failure to discharge any duty required by law

A. 1 only is correct.

B. 2 only is correct.

C. Both 1 and 2 are correct.

D. Both 1 and 2 are not correct.

21. An appeal from a decision regarding a notary commission goes to which court?

A. Town Appeals Court

B. County Appeals Court

C. Appellate Division of the Superior Court

D. none of the above

MULTIPLE CHOICE ANS. CH. 5: COMMISSION DENIAL. REVOCATION, SUSPENSION...

19.

C. State Treasurer

The **State Treasurer** may deny a notary public commission if the applicant committed an incompetent or dishonest act which demonstrates that the applicant does not have the competence or reliability necessary to be a notary public.

20.

C. Both 1 and 2 are correct.

A person may be denied a notary public commission due to:

1) conviction of a crime of the second degree or above

2) failure to discharge any duty required by law

21.

C. Appellate Division of the Superior Court

An appeal from a decision regarding a notary commission goes to the Appellate Division of the Superior Court.

MULTIPLE CHOICE QUESTIONS

22.

Which of the following statements is not correct?

A. A notarial act is evidenced by a certificate and a stamp.

B. Certificates may be executed days after the notarial act.

C. The notary signs and dates the notarial certificate.

D. A notarial certificate must state the jurisdiction where the notarial act is performed.

23.

Which of the following is correct?

A. A notarial certificate must state the date of birth of the notary.

B. A notarial certificate may be executed days after the notarial act.

C. A notarial certificate must state the date of expiration of the notary's commission.

D. A notary is not required to sign the notarial certificate.

24.

The notary public official stamp must include which of the following?

A. the age of the notary

B. the date of birth of the notary

C. the name of the notary

D. the home address of the notary

MULTIPLE CHOICE ANSWERS

22.

B. Certificates may be executed days after the notarial act.

This statement is **NOT** correct. Certificates must be executed **at the same time** (contemporaneously) as the notarial act.

23.

C. A notarial certificate must state the date of expiration of the notary's commission. (This is the only correct statement.)

The other 3 statements are not correct because:

The certificate does **NOT** have to state the date of birth of the notary.

The certificate must be executed at the time as the notarial act.

A notary **MUST** sign the notarial certificate.

24.

C. the name of the notary

The notary public official stamp must include the name of the notary.

MULTIPLE CHOICE QUESTIONS

25.

In what location on the document page must the official stamp be affixed?

A. at the beginning of the document

B. near the signature of the notary public

C. anywhere on the document

D. on a separate page of the document

26.

Which of the following statements is not correct?

A. A notary is responsible for keeping a notary stamp secure.

B. Generally, a notary public cannot allow another person to use his stamp.

C. If an employer pays for a notary public device, the device becomes the property of the employer.

D. A notary stamp must include the title "Notary Public, State of New Jersey."

27.

If a notary stamping device is stolen, the notary must inform the State Treasurer within _____ calendar days.

A. 5

B. 10

C. 15

D. 30

MULTIPLE CHOICE ANSWERS

25.

B. near the signature of the notary public

The official stamp must be affixed near the signature of the notary public.

26.

C. If an employer pays for a notary public device, then the device is the property of the employer.

(This statement is **NOT** correct because the notary public device is the property of the notary public, regardless of who paid for it.)

27.

B. 10 DAYS

If a notary stamping device is stolen, the notary must inform the State Treasurer within **10 (TEN)** calendar days.

MULTIPLE CHOICE QUESTIONS

28. Must a notary maintain separate journals for tangible and electronic notarial acts?

A. Yes, in all cases.

B. Yes, only if the notary executes a document out of county.

C. Yes if the notary is commissioned after 2022.

D. No. One journal must be kept.

29. Choose the best answer. A journal maintained in a tangible medium must be:

1) in a permanent medium only

2) bound medium only

A. 1 only

B. 2 only

C. both 1 and 2

D. neither 1 nor 2

30. Which of the following choices is not correct? The notary journal must contain:

A. the date and time of the notarial act.

B. the type of notarial act.

C. the name of each person for whom a notarial act was performed.

D. the age of each person for whom a notarial act was performed.

MULTIPLE CHOICE ANSWERS

28.

D. No. One journal must be kept.

A notary must maintain **ONE** JOURNAL at a time to record **both** tangible and electronic notarial acts.

29.

C. both 1 and 2

A journal maintained in a tangible medium must be <u>BOTH</u> in a permanent medium <u>and</u> in a bound medium.

30

D. the age of each person for whom a notarial act was performed.

The notary journal does **NOT** have to contain the age of each person for whom a notarial act was performed.

MULTIPLE CHOICE QUESTIONS

31.

If the notary journal is stolen or lost, the notary must notify the State Treasurer within _____ (at the State Treasurer's online site).

A. 5 days

B. 10 days

C. 15 days

D. 30 days

32.

A notary must retain her journal for _____ years after the notarial act.

A. 3

B. 7

C. 10

D. 12

33.

The fees charged for a notarial act:

A. do not have to be recorded in the notary journal.

B. may be recorded as one total sum.

C. must be recorded individually.

D. none of the above.

MULTIPLE CHOICE ANSWERS

31.

B. 10 days

If the notary journal is stolen or lost, the notary must notify the State Treasurer within **10 DAYS** (at the State Treasurer's online site).

32.

C. 10

A notary must retain her journal for **10 (TEN) years** after the notarial act.

33.

C. must be recorded individually.

The fees charged for a notarial act must be recorded individually.

MULTIPLE CHOICE QUESTIONS

34.

Choose the best answer. Which of the following statements are correct regarding a notary journal maintained in a tangible medium?

A. The journal must be in a permanent form.

B. The journal must be in a bound register.

C. Both A and B are correct statements.

D. Both A and B are false statements

35.

Choose the best answer. Which of the following statements are correct regarding a notary journal maintained in an electronic medium? If a notary journal is maintained in an electronic format, it must be:

A. in a permanent format.

B. in a tamper-evident format .

C. Both A and B are correct statements.

D. Both A and B are false statements

36.

Which of the following is not correct? The notary journal must contain:

A. the date of the notarial act

B. the time of the notarial act

C. the type of notarial act

D. the social security number of the notary

MULTIPLE CHOICE ANSWERS

34.

C. Both A and B are correct statements.

A notary journal maintained in a tangible medium must be in a permanent form **AND** must be in a bound register.

35.

C. Both A and B are correct statements.

If a notary journal is maintained in an electronic format, it must be in a permanent format **AND** must be in a tamper-evident format.

36

D. the social security number of the notary

The social security number of the notary public is **NOT** part of the notary journal.

MULTIPLE CHOICE QUESTIONS

37. Which of the following two choices are correct? The notary journal must contain:

A. the name of each person for whom a notarial act was performed.

B. the height of each person for whom a notarial act was performed.

C. Both are correct.

D. Both are not correct.

38. If the notary knows an individual because of personal knowledge, what must the notary record in the journal?

A. that no notarization is required

B. that no fee was charged

C. the number of years of acquaintance

D. a statement to that effect

39. If the notary identified an individual by an identity document (ID) the notary must record in the journal the date of issuance and _____ of the identity document.

A. date of expiration

B. date of reissuance

C. date of creation

D. none of the above

MULTIPLE CHOICE ANSWERS

37.

A. the name of each person for whom a notarial act was performed.

The notary journal must contain the name of each person for whom a notarial act was performed. Height is **not** required.

38.

D. a statement to that effect

If the notary knows an individual because of personal knowledge, the notary must record in the journal a statement to that effect.

39.

A. date of expiration

If the notary identified an individual by an identity document (ID) the notary must record in the journal the date of issuance and **date of expiration** of the identity document.

MULTIPLE CHOICE QUESTIONS

40.

Which fees must a notary record in the notarial journal?

A. Fees greater than $10 only.

B. Fees greater than $15 only.

C. Fees greater than $20 only.

D. none of the above.

41.

If the notary journal is stolen or lost, the notary must notify the State Treasurer within _____ (at the State Treasurer's online site).

A. 5 days

B. 10 days

C. 15 days

D. 30 days

42.

A notary must retain her journal for _____ after the notarial act.

A. 1 year

B. 2 years

C. 3 years

D. 10 years

MULTIPLE CHOICE ANSWERS

40.

D. none of the above.

A notary MUST record in the notarial journal an **itemized list of fees charged** for the notarial act (regardless of the total amount charged).

41.

B. 10 days

If the notary journal is stolen or lost, the notary must notify the State Treasurer within **10 (TEN) days** (at the State Treasurer's online site).

42.

D. 10 years

A notary must retain her journal for **10 (TEN) years** after the notarial act.

MULTIPLE CHOICE QUESTIONS

43. If a notary dies or becomes incompetent, the representative must contact the State Treasurer within _____ days for instructions on how to submit the notary journal to the State Treasurer.

A. 10 days

B. 30 days

C. 45 days

D. 60 days

44. _____ who is a notary may instead of maintaining a notary journal maintain a record of notarial acts in his office files.

A. a secretary

B. an attorney

C. a legal assistant

D. none of the above

45. The fees charged for a notarial act:

A. may be recorded in a notary journal as one sum amount.

B. are not required to be recorded in a notarial journal.

C. must be itemized in a notarial journal.

D. none of the above

MULTIPLE CHOICE ANSWERS

43.

C. 45 days

If a notary dies or becomes incompetent, the representative must contact the State Treasurer within **45 DAYS** for instructions on how to submit the notary journal to the State Treasurer.

44.

B. an attorney

An attorney who is a notary may instead of maintaining a notary journal, maintain a record of notarial acts in his office files.

45.

C. must be itemized in a notarial journal.

The fees charged for a notarial act **must be itemized in a notarial journal**.

CHAPTER 7 QUICK QUESTIONS: FORMS OF ID AND COPY CERTIFICATION

46.
Chose the best answer. A notary may satisfy herself as to the identity of an individual by _____.

A. personal knowledge

B. satisfactory evidence

C. Both A and B

D. Neither A nor B.

47.
Choose the best answer. Valid forms of satisfactory evidence of identity include:

A. a passport

B. a driver's license

C. government-issued, non-driver ID card

D. all of the above

48.
A government issued non-driver identification card is valid ID if not expired more than _____ before the notarial act.

A. one year

B. two years

C. three years

D. none of the above

CHAPTER 7 QUICK ANSWERS: FORMS OF ID AND COPY CERTIFICATION

46.

C. Both A and B

A notary may satisfy herself as to the identity of an individual by **personal knowledge or by satisfactory evidence**.

47.

D. all of the above

Valid forms of satisfactory evidence of identity include a **passport, driver's license, or government-issued, non-driver ID card**.

48.

C. three years

A government issued non-driver identification card is valid ID if not expired more than **3 (THREE) years** before the notarial act.

CHAPTER 8 MULTIPLE CHOICE QUESTIONS: USE OF COMMUNICATION TECHNOLOGY

49.

A systems that uses fingerprints, facial, and voice patterns to identify a person is referred to as a _____ identification system.

A. lithographic

B. photographic

C. volumetric

D. biometric

50.

A "Digital Public key certificate" is which of the following?

A. photo ID

B. electronic credential

C. photocopy code

D. none of the above

51.

Which of the following is referred to as a "foreign state?"

A. a U.S. state

B. an Indian tribe

C. the United States

D. none of the above

CHAPTER 8 MULTIPLE CHOICE ANSWERS: USE OF COMMUNICATION TECHNOLOGY

49.

D. biometric

A systems that uses fingerprints, facial, and voice patterns to identify a person is referred to as a **biometric** identification system.

50.

B. electronic credential

A "Digital Public key certificate" is an **electronic credential**.

51.

D. none of the above

A political entity (**other** than a U.S. state, an Indian tribe, or the United States) is known as a "**foreign**" state.

MULTIPLE CHOICE QUESTIONS

52. A notary who intends on doing remote notarization must notify the _____ _____ before doing any remote notarization.

A. Secretary of State

B. State Controller

C. State Treasurer

D. County Clerk

53. A notarial act that is done using remote technology for a person who is located in a remote location is considered done in New Jersey and is governed by _____ law.

A. New Jersey

B. U.S.

C. federal

D. international

54. For remote notarization, the person:

A. must be located in a New Jersey county

B. must be located in a New Jersey city

C. does not have to be located within the state of New Jersey.

D. none of the above are correct

MULTIPLE CHOICE ANSWERS

52.

C. State Treasurer

A notary who intends on doing remote notarization must notify the **State Treasurer** before doing any remote notarization.

53.

A. New Jersey

A notarial act that is done using remote technology for a person that is located in a remote location is considered done in New Jersey and is governed by **New Jersey** law.

54.

C. does NOT have to be located within the state of New Jersey.

For remote notarization, the person does NOT have to be located within the state of New Jersey.

CHAPTER 9 MULTIPLE CHOICE QUESTIONS: ELECTRONIC NOTARIZATION

55.

To be considered reliable, an electronic signature and stamp must be:

A. generic.

B. purchased in an authorized legal stationery store.

C. unique to the notarial officer.

D. none of the above

56.

Which of the following choices is not correct? A notarial officer may refuse to perform a notarial act for a person that:

A. is not competent

B. did not sign the document

C. is over the age of 65.

D. has a guardian appointed for him.

57.

For administering oaths, taking affidavits, taking proofs of a deed, and taking acknowledgements the fee is $_____ per act.

A. $2.00

B. $2.50

C. $15.00

D. $25.00

CHAPTER 9 MULTIPLE CHOICE ANSWERS: ELECTRONIC NOTARIZATION

55.

C. unique to the notarial officer.

To be considered reliable, an electronic signature and stamp must be unique to the notarial officer.

56.

C. is over the age of 65.

A notarial officer may **NOT** refuse to perform a notarial act solely for the reason that a person is over the age of 65.

57.

B. $2.50

For administering oaths, taking affidavits, taking proofs of a deed, and taking acknowledgements the fee is **$2.50** per act.

MULTIPLE CHOICE QUESTIONS

58. Fee for administering oaths, taking affidavits, taking proofs of a deed, and taking acknowledgments of the grantors in the transfer of real estate, regardless of the number of such services performed in a single transaction to transfer real estate is:

A. $15.00

B. $20.00

C. $25.00

D. none of the above

59. Fee for administering oaths, taking affidavits, and taking acknowledgments of the mortgagors in the financing of real estate, regardless of the number of such services performed in a single transaction to finance real estate is:

A. $15.00

B. $20.00

C. $25.00

D. none of the above

60. A notary performs three notarial acts (takes an acknowledgment, administers an oath, and takes an affidavit). What is the total fee that the notary can collect?

A. $2.50

B. $7.50

C. $15.00

D. $25.00

MULTIPLE CHOICE ANSWERS

58.

A. $15.00

Fee for administering oaths, taking affidavits, taking proofs of a deed, and taking acknowledgments of the grantors in the **transfer of real estate**, regardless of the number of such services performed in a single transaction to transfer real estate is **$15.00**.

59.

C. $25.00

Fee for administering oaths, taking affidavits, and taking acknowledgments of the mortgagors in the **financing of real estate,** regardless of the number of such services performed in a single transaction to finance real estate is **$25.00**.

60.

B. $7.50

The fee for administering oaths, taking affidavits, taking proofs of a deed, and taking acknowledgements is **$2.50 per act**. Therefore, the amount that can be collected for the 3 notarial acts is $2.50 X 3 = **$7.50**.

LEGAL TERMS

The following are useful legal terms. They contain editorial comments intended to jump-start your understanding of the words. For official definitions, please consult a legal dictionary.

Acknowledgment – is a declaration made before an official (example: notary public) that under the person's free act and deed he did execute the instrument.

Administrator – An administrator of an estate is appointed by the court which empowers him to manage the affairs of the dead person. The court appoints an administrator where a person dies without leaving a will or leaves a will without naming an executor.

Affiant – An affidavit (a sworn to or affirmed written statement) is signed by a person called the affiant.

Affidavit – is a signed statement that is sworn to by the person signing it. An affidavit is sworn to in front of a notary public or other officer with authority to administer an oath.

Affirmation – A person who does not want to take an oath (because of religious, ethical, or other reasons) may **affirm** as to the truthfulness of his statements. The act of affirming is called the affirmation. An affirmation is just as binding as an oath.

Apostille – An apostille is an authentication of a notarized document. It is issued by the New Jersey Department of the Treasury. It may be used internationally.

Attest – To attest is to be present at the execution of a written instrument and also to subscribe (sign) the written instrument as a witness to the execution of the instrument.

Attestation clause – As it refers to wills, an attestation clause is the written portion at the end of a will where the witnesses attest that the will was executed in front of them and also state the procedural manner of the execution of the will.

Bill of sale – A bill of sale is a written document that is given by the vendor (seller of personal property) to the vendee (buyer). It passes title from the vendor to the vendee.

Chattel – Chattel means property that is personal in nature, such as household goods. Chattel does NOT include real property (land, buildings).

Chattel paper – A written obligation to pay money for specific personal goods is known as chattel paper

Codicil – As it relates to wills, a codicil is an attachment to a will that adds to or changes (modifies) the will in some way.

Consideration – is what is given in value to induce someone to enter into a contract. Consideration examples are: property, money, services, etc.

Contempt of court – are actions which hinder the execution of court orders and display disrespect of court's authority.

Contract – A contract (an agreement between parties) can be oral or written. For there to be a contract, there must be legal consideration to enter into the contract.

Conveyance – The instrument which creates, assigns, transfers, or surrenders an interest in <u>real</u> property is called a conveyance.

Deponent – Deponent means the same as affiant. A deponent (affiant) is a person who signs the deposition and makes an oath to a written statement.

Deposition – A deposition is testimony taken before an authorized official (such as a notary public). It is taken out of court with the intention of using it at a hearing or trial.

Duress – Duress means exercising unlawful constraint on a person with the intention of forcing him to do certain acts which may be against the person's will.

Escrow – is depositing an instrument with a person who on the occurrence of an event must give the instrument to a designated person. Escrow is often used during the sale of a building.

Executor – is a person designated (named) in a will to carry out the instructions of the deceased that are stated in the will.

Ex Parte (one sided) – A court proceeding is ex parte (one sided) when it is conducted with only one of the parties being present (plaintiff or defendant).

Felony – A felony is an offense for which a sentence of imprisonment of more than a year (or death) may be imposed.

Guardian – A guardian is a person in charge of another person's property or person (usually relates to guardians of minors).

Judgment – A judgment declares the rights of individuals, including a judgment that one party owes money to another and specifying the amount owed.

Jurat – A jurat is the section of an affidavit which contains the certification of the notary public that the document was sworn to in front of the notary public.

Laches – is the negligence or delay in the assertion of a legal right. The concept of laches may be used as a defense in certain legal proceedings, such as in proceedings for unpaid rent.

Lease – Lease is a contract regarding the right to the possession of real property (land or buildings). It is made for consideration (rent, lease payments) and transfers the right to possession of real property for a period of time.

Lien – A lien is the attachment of a legal claim on property until the debt on the property is satisfied.

Litigation – is the process of pursuing a lawsuit.

Misdemeanor – A crime that is not a felony. Misdemeanors are less serious than felonies and are punishable by a sentence of imprisonment up to and including a year.

Mortgage on real property – A written instrument that is used to create a lien on real property until the debt is paid.

Notary public – is a public officer who among other things is authorized to administer oaths and affirmations relating to the truth of statements and authorized to execute acknowledgments of deeds or writings which may thereafter be admitted into evidence.

Oath – An <u>oath</u> or <u>affirmation</u> is a verbal pledge of the truthfulness of the statements made.

Plaintiff – A plaintiff is the party who starts a civil lawsuit.

Power of attorney – is a statement in writing by a person which gives another person the power to act for him.

Proof – as it relates to the witnessing of the execution of instruments means the formal declaration of the witness that he witnessed the execution of the instrument. The witness must state his residence and that he knew the person signing the instrument.

Protest – written statement by a notary that a promissory note or bill of exchange was presented for acceptance or payment was refused.

Signature of notary public – Notary must sign his name (same name as under which appointed).

Statute – is a law that was created by the legislature.

Statute of limitations - law which prescribe the time during which a civil action or criminal prosecution must be commenced.

Subordination clause – A clause in an agreement (contract) which allows a future mortgage to take priority over an existing mortgage.

Swear – any mode of oath administration that is authorized by law.

Taking an acknowledgment – includes:
1. person who is named in the instrument informing the notary that he is that person and that he indeed did execute the instrument
2. the act of the notary checking the identity of the person

Venue – is the geographical area where the affidavit or acknowledgment is taken by notary.

Will – the instrument in which a person sets forth his wishes relating to the disposition of his property after his death.

PRACTICE TEST 1

1. Fee for administering oaths, taking affidavits, taking proofs of a deed, and taking acknowledgments of the grantors in the transfer of real estate, regardless of the number of such services performed in a single transaction to transfer real estate is:

A. $15.00

B. $20.00

C. $25.00

D. $35.00

2. For administering oaths, taking affidavits, taking proofs of a deed, and taking acknowledgements the fee is $_____ per act.

A. $2.00

B. $2.50

C. $15.00

D. none of the above

3. Which of the following choices is not correct? A notarial officer may refuse to perform a notarial act for a person that:

A. is over the age of 75.

B. has a guardian appointed for him.

C. is not competent.

D. did not sign the document.

4. Which of the following statements is correct? For remote notarization, the person:

A. must be located in a New Jersey county.

B. must be located in a New Jersey city.

C. does not have to be located within the state of New Jersey.

D. must be a person with disabilities.

5. A notarial act that is done using remote technology for a person that is located in a remote location is considered done in New Jersey and is governed by _____ law.

A. federal

B. international

C. New Jersey

D. U.S.

6. A notary who intends on doing remote notarization must notify the _____ _____ before doing any remote notarization.

A. State Treasurer

B. County Clerk

C. Secretary of State

D. State Controller

7. Which of the following is referred to as a "foreign state?"

A. a U.S. state

B. an Indian tribe

C. the United States

D. Canada

8. Which of the following is an "electronic credential?"

A. photo ID

B. Digital Public Key Certificate

C. photocopy code

D. none of the above

9. A systems that uses fingerprints, facial, and voice patterns to identify a person is referred to as a _____ identification system.

A. lithographic

B. biometric

C. photographic

D. volumetric

10. A government issued non-driver identification card is valid ID if not expired more than _____ before the notarial act.

A. 6 months

B. 1 year

C. 2 years

D. 3 years

11. Valid forms of satisfactory evidence of identity does not include which of the following?

A. a passport

B. a driver's license

C. government-issued, non- driver ID card

D. a birth certificate

12. Choose the best answer. A notary may satisfy herself as to the identity of an individual by _____.

A. personal knowledge

B. satisfactory evidence

C. personal assurance by the individual being identified

D. Both A and B

13. A(n) _____ who is a notary may instead of maintaining a notary journal maintain a journal of notarial acts in his office files.

A. secretary and real estate broker

B. attorney

C. legal assistant

D. none of the above

14. Which fees must a notary record in the notary journal?

A. Fees greater than $10 only.

B. Fees greater than $15 only.

C. Fees greater than $20 only.

D. All fees individually

15. If the notary identified an individual by an identity document (ID) the notary must record in the notary journal the date of issuance and _____ of the identity document.

A. date of creation

B. the age of the person of the identity document

C. date of expiration

D. date of reissuance

16. If the notary knows an individual because of personal knowledge, what must the notary record in the notary journal?

A. that no notarization is required.

B. that no fee was charged.

C. the number of years of acquaintance.

D. none of the above

17. Choose the best answer. Which of the following two choices are correct? The notary journal must contain:

A. the name of each person for whom a notarial act was performed.

B. the method used by notary to identify the person for whom the notarial act was performed.

C. Both are correct.

D. Both are not correct.

18. The fees charged for a notarial act:

A. must be recorded individually.

B. do not have to be recorded in the notary journal if less than $15..

C. may be recorded as one total sum.

D. none of the above.

19. A notary must retain her notary journal for _____ year(s) after the notarial act.

A. 3

B. 7

C. 10

D. 12

20. If the notary journal is stolen or lost, the notary must notify the State Treasurer within _____ (at the State Treasurer's online site).

A. 5 days

B. 7 days

C. 10 days

D. 30 days

21. Which of the following choices is not correct? The notary journal must contain:

A. the date and time of the notarial act

B. the type of notarial act

C. the name of each person for whom a notarial act was performed

D. the name of the clerk of county

22. Which of 2 choices are correct? A notary journal maintained in a tangible medium must be:

  1) in a permanent medium

  2) in a looseleaf medium

A. 1 only is correct

B. 2 only is correct

C. Both 1 and 2 are correct.

D. Neither 1 nor 2 are correct.

23. Must a notary maintain separate notary journals for tangible and electronic notarizations?

A. Yes, in all cases.

B. Yes, only if the notary executes a document out of county.

C. Yes if the notary is commissioned after 2022.

D. none of the above.

24. If a notary stamping device is stolen, the notary must inform the State Treasurer within _____ calendar days.

A. 10   C. 30

B. 15   D. none of the above

25. Which of the following statements is not correct?

A. A notary is not responsible for keeping a notary stamp secure.

B. Generally, a notary public cannot allow another person to use his stamp.

C. If an employer pays for a notary public device, the device does not become the property of the employer.

D. A notary stamp must include the title "Notary Public, State of New Jersey."

26. In what location on the document page must the official stamp be affixed?

A. near the signatures of the attorneys

B. on the cover page of the document

C. at the beginning of the document

D. near the signature of the notary public

27. The notary public official stamp must include which of the following?

A. the age of the notary

B. the date of birth of the notary

C. the nickname of the notary

D. the expiration date of the commission

28. Which of the following is correct?

A. A notarial certificate must state the date of birth of the notary.

B. A notarial certificate must be executed at the same time as the notarial act.

C. A notarial certificate must state the date of issuance of the notary's commission.

D. A notary is not required to sign the notarial certificate.

29. Which of the following statements is not correct?

A. The principal signs and dates the notarial certificate.

B. A notarial certificate must state the jurisdiction where the notarial act is performed.

C. A notarial act is evidenced by a certificate and a stamp.

D. Certificates are executed at the same time as the notarial act.

30. An appeal from a decision regarding a notary commission goes to which court?

A. Town Appeals Court

B. County Appeals Court

C. City Court

D. none of the above

31. Which of the following two choices are correct? A person may be denied a notary public commission due to:

   1) conviction of a felony of the second degree or above

   2) conviction of any offense

A. 1 only is correct

B. 2 only is correct

C. Both 1 and 2 are correct.

D. Both 1 and 2 are not correct.

32. The _____ may deny a notary public commission if the applicant committed an incompetent or dishonest act which demonstrates that the applicant does not have the competence or reliability necessary to be a notary public.

A. County Clerk

B. State Controller

C. Attorney General

D. none of the above

33. A notary who changes her name from the one she was commissioned shall notify the _____ and specify the circumstances of the name change.

A. State Treasurer

B. County Clerk

C. State Controller

D. none of the above

34. The _____ must cancel and revoke a notary commission if oath is not taken within 3 months of receipt of the commission.

A. State Treasurer

B. State Controller

C. Attorney General

D. none of the above

35. A resident or nonresident notary shall take an oath within _____ of receipt of original or renewal commission before the county clerk.

A. 1 month

B. 2 months

C. 3 months

D. none of the above

36. What is the maximum fee that the State Treasurer can charge for each test administered online?

A. $10

B. $20

C. $25

D. none of the above

37. The fee for the notary public application commission is:

A. $10

B. $20

C. $35

D. $25

38. Choose the best answer. Which of the following applications must be sent electronically to the State Treasurer?

A. application for a notary public commission

B. renewal application for a notary public commission

C. both A and B.

D. neither A nor B.

39. Which of the following statements is correct? A notary public may advertise that he is an attorney:

A. if he is a law school enrollee.

B. if he has had some legal experience in New Jersey.

C. if he has worked as a legal assistant in a law firm.

D. none of the above

40. If a notary advertises in another language, he must include in the same advertisement a notice that:

   1) he is not an attorney

   2) he provides immigration legal advice.

A. 1 only

B. 2 only

C. both 1 and 2

D. neither 1 nor 2

41. Which of the following notarial acts are voidable?

   1) a notarial act where the notary does not have a direct interest

   2) a notarial act where the spouse of the notary is a party

A. number 1 only

B. number 2 only

C. both 1 and 2

D. neither 1 nor 2

42. A notary public commissioned in New Jersey may perform his duties:

A. in his state of birth and county of residence only.

B. only in the county where he is commissioned.

C. only in the county of birth and adjoining counties.

D. throughout the State of New Jersey.

43. Which of the following is not correct? To be commissioned a notary in New Jersey, a person may be the following:

A. a resident of New Jersey

B. employed in New Jersey

C. an attorney practicing in New Jersey

D. a legal secretary of the age of 17.

44. The minimum age to be a notary public in the State of New Jersey is:

A. 16   C. 18

B. 17   D. 21

45. Choose the best answer. To "sign" a document means which of the following?

A. to execute a tangible record.

B. to associate with an electronic record an electronic symbol.

C. to execute an oral contract

D. both A and B

46. Which of the following is the government officials who is empowered to commission notaries?

A. the Governor

B. the Commerce Commissioner

C. the State Treasurer

D. the Controller

47. Which of the following is a notarial act?

A. acting as a guardian

B. taking a verification

C. acting as an executor of an estate

D. none of the above

48. Acting as an authorized representative of another person is described as which of the following?

A. acting fraudulently

B. acting without established authority

C. acting in a representative capacity

D. none of the above

49. A document may be:

A. physical (tangible) or electronic

B. electronic only.

C. physical (tangible) only

D. none of the above choices are correct.

50. "_____" is defined as a declaration made in front of a notary public that the person has signed a document, and if the person signed in a representative capacity, that the person had the authority to sign it.

A. affidavit

B. acknowledgment

C. compliance

D. contract

TEST 1 ANSWER KEY

1.	A	11.	D	21.	D	31.	A	41.	B
2.	B	12.	D	22.	A	32.	D	42.	D
3.	A	13.	B	23.	D	33.	A	43.	D
4.	C	14.	D	24.	A	34.	A	44.	C
5.	C	15.	C	25.	A	35.	C	45.	D
6.	A	16.	D	26.	D	36.	D	46.	C
7.	D	17.	C	27.	D	37.	D	47.	B
8.	B	18.	A	28.	B	38.	C	48.	C
9.	B	19.	C	29.	A	39.	D	49.	A
10.	D	20.	C	30.	D	40.	A	50.	B

ANSWERS: PRACTICE TEST 1

1. Fee for administering oaths, taking affidavits, taking proofs of a deed, and taking acknowledgments of the grantors in the transfer of real estate, regardless of the number of such services performed in a single transaction to transfer real estate is:

A. **$15.00**

B. $20.00

C. $25.00

D. $35.00

1. Answer: **A. $15.00**

Fee for administering oaths, taking affidavits, taking proofs of a deed, and taking acknowledgments of the grantors in the **transfer of real estate**, regardless of the number of such services performed in a single transaction to transfer real estate is **$15.00**.

NOTE ALSO that the fee for administering oaths, taking affidavits, and taking acknowledgments of the mortgagors in the **financing of real estate**, regardless of the number of such services performed in a single transaction to finance real estate is **$25.00**.

----

2. For administering oaths, taking affidavits, taking proofs of a deed, and taking acknowledgements the fee is $_____ per act.

A. $2.00

B. **$2.50**

C. $15.00

D. none of the above

2. Answer: **B. $2.50**

For administering oaths, taking affidavits, taking proofs of a deed, and taking acknowledgements the fee is **$2.50** per act.

----

3. Which of the following choices is **not** correct? A notarial officer may refuse to perform a notarial act for a person that:

A. **is over the age of 75.**

B. has a guardian appointed for him.

C. is not competent

D. did not sign the document

3. Answer: **A. is over the age of 75.**

A notarial officer may **NOT** refuse to perform a notarial act solely for the reason that a person is over the age of 75.

----

4. Which of the following statements is correct? For remote notarization, the person:

A. must be located in a New Jersey county

B. must be located in a New Jersey city

C. does not have to be located within the state of New Jersey.

D. must be a person with disabilities

4. Answer: **C. does NOT have to be located within the state of New Jersey.**

For remote notarization, the person does **NOT** have to be located within the state of New Jersey.

----

5. A notarial act that is done using remote technology for a person that is located in a remote location is considered done in New Jersey and is governed by _____ law.

A. federal

B. international

C. New Jersey

D. U.S.

5. Answer: **C. New Jersey**

A notarial act that is done using remote technology for a person that is located in a remote location is considered done in New Jersey and is governed by **New Jersey** law.

----

6. A notary who intends on doing remote notarization must notify the _____ _____ before doing any remote notarization.

A. State Treasurer

B. County Clerk

C. Secretary of State

D. State Controller

6. Answer: **A. State Treasurer**

A notary who intends on doing remote notarization must notify the **State Treasurer** before doing any remote notarization.

----

7. Which of the following is referred to as a "foreign state?"

A. a U.S. state

B. an Indian tribe

C. the United States

D. Canada

7. Answer: **D. Canada**

A political entity (**other** than a U.S. state, an Indian tribe, or the United States) is known as a "**foreign**" state.

----

8. Which of the following is an "electronic credential?"

A. photo ID

B. Digital Public Key Certificate

C. photocopy code

D. none of the above

8. Answer: **B. Digital Public key certificate**

A "Digital Public key certificate" is an **electronic credential**.

----

9. A systems that uses fingerprints, facial, and voice patterns to identify a person is referred to as a _____ identification system.

A. lithographic

B. biometric

C. photographic

D. volumetric

9. Answer: **B. biometric**

A systems that uses fingerprints, facial, and voice patterns to identify a person is referred to as a **biometric** identification system.

----

10. A government issued non-driver identification card is valid ID if not expired more than _____ before the notarial act.

A. 6 months

B. 1 year

C. 2 years

D. 3 years

10. Answer: **D. 3 years**

A government issued non-driver identification card is valid ID if not expired more than **3 (THREE) years** before the notarial act.

----

11. Valid forms of satisfactory evidence of identity does **not** include which of the following?

A. a passport

B. a driver's license

C. government-issued, non- driver ID card

D. a birth certificate

11. **D. a birth certificate**

A birth certificate is **not** a document that can be used by itself as valid ID.

----

12. Choose the best answer. A notary may satisfy herself as to the identity of an individual by _____.

A. personal knowledge

B. satisfactory evidence

C. personal assurance by the individual

D. Both A and B

12. Answer: **D. Both A and B**

A notary may satisfy herself as to the identity of an individual by personal knowledge, and satisfactory evidence.

----

13. A(n)_____ who is a notary may instead of maintaining a notary journal maintain a record of notarial acts in his office files.

A. secretary and real estate broker

B. attorney

C. legal assistant

D. none of the above

13. Answer: **B. an attorney**

An attorney who is a notary may instead of maintaining a notary journal maintain a record of notarial acts in his office files.

----

14. Which fees must a notary record in the notary journal?

A. Fees greater than $10 only.

B. Fees greater than $15 only.

C. Fees greater than $20 only.

D. All fees individually

Answer: **D. All fees individually**

A notary must record **individually all fees** in the notary journal.

----

15. If the notary identified an individual by an identity document (ID) the notary must record in the notary journal the date of issuance and _____ of the identity document.

A. date of creation

B. the age of the person of the identity document

C. date of expiration

D. date of reissuance

15. Answer: **C. date of expiration**

If the notary identified an individual by an identity document (ID) the notary must record in the notary journal the date of issuance and **date of expiration** of the identity document.

----

16. If the notary knows an individual because of personal knowledge, what must the notary record in the notary journal?

A. that no notarization is required.

B. that no fee was charged.

C. the number of years of acquaintance.

D. none of the above

16. Answer: **D. none of the above**

If the notary knows an individual because of personal knowledge, the notary must record in the notary journal **a statement to that effect.**

----

17. Choose the best answer. Which of the following two choices are correct? The notary journal must contain:

A. the name of each person for whom a notarial act was performed.

B. the method used by notary to identify the person for whom the notarial act was performed.

C. Both are correct.

D. Both are not correct.

17. Answer: **C. Both are correct.**

The notary journal must contain the name of each person for whom a notarial act was performed, AND the method used by notary to identify the person for whom the notarial act was performed.

----

18. The fees charged for a notarial act:

A. must be recorded individually.

B. do not have to be recorded in the notary journal if less than $15..

C. may be recorded as one total sum.

D. none of the above.

18. Answer: **A. must be recorded individually.**

The fees charged for a notarial act must be recorded individually.

----

19. A notary must retain her notary journal for _____ year(s) after the notarial act.

A. 3

B. 7

C. 10

D. 12

19. Answer: **C 10**

A notary must retain her notary journal for **10 (TEN) years** after the notarial act.

----

20. If the notary journal is stolen or lost, the notary must notify the State Treasurer within _____ (at the State Treasurer's online site).

A. 5 days

B. 7 days

C. 10 days

D. 30 days

20. Answer: **C. 10 days**

If the notary journal is stolen or lost, the notary must notify the State Treasurer within **10 DAYS** (at the State Treasurer's online site).

----

21. Which of the following choices is **not** correct? The notary journal must contain:

A. the date and time of the notarial act

B. the type of notarial act

C. the name of each person for whom a notarial act was performed

D. the name of the clerk of county

21. Answer: **D. the name of the clerk of county**.

The notary journal does **NOT** have to contain the name of the clerk of county.

----

22. Which of 2 choices are correct? A notary journal maintained in a tangible medium must be:

   1) in a permanent medium

   2) in a looseleaf medium

A. 1 only is correct

B. 2 only is correct

C. Both 1 and 2 are correct.

D. Neither 1 nor 2 are correct.

22. Answer: **A. 1 only is correct**.

A notary journal maintained in a tangible medium must be 1) in a permanent medium AND **2) bound medium** (not a looseleaf medium)**.**

----

23. Must a notary maintain separate notary journals for tangible and electronic notarizations?

A. Yes, in all cases.

B. Yes, only if the notary executes a document out of county.

C. Yes if the notary is commissioned after 2022.

D. none of the above.

23. Answer: **D. none of the above.**

In all cases, **ONE** notary journal for both tangible and electronic notarizations must be kept.

----

24. If a notary stamping device is stolen, the notary must inform the State Treasurer within ____ calendar days.

A. 10

B. 15

C. 30

D. none of the above

24. Answer: **A. 10**

If a notary stamping device is stolen, the notary must inform the State Treasurer within **10 (TEN) calendar days**.

----

25. Which of the following statements is **not** correct?

A. A notary is not responsible for keeping a notary stamp secure.

B. Generally, a notary public cannot allow another person to use his stamp.

C. If an employer pays for a notary public device, the device does not become the property of the employer.

D. A notary stamp must include the title "Notary Public, State of New Jersey."

25. Answer: **A. A notary is not responsible for keeping a notary stamp secure.**

Choice "A" is not correct because a notary **IS RESPONSIBLE** for keeping the notary stamp secure.

----

26. In what location on the document page must the official stamp be affixed?

A. near the signatures of the attorneys

B. on the cover page of the document

C. at the beginning of the document

D. near the signature of the notary public

26. Answer: **D. near the signature of the notary public**

The official stamp must be affixed near the signature of the notary public.

----

27. The notary public official stamp must include which of the following?

A. the age of the notary

B. the date of birth of the notary

C. the nickname of the notary

D. the expiration date of the commission

27. Answer: **D. the expiration date of the commission**

The notary public official stamp must include the expiration date of the commission.

----

28. Which of the following is correct?

A. A notarial certificate must state the date of birth of the notary.

B. A notarial certificate must be executed at the same time as the notarial act.

C. A notarial certificate must state the date of issuance of the notary's commission.

D. A notary is not required to sign the notarial certificate.

28. Answer: **B. A notarial certificate must be executed at the same time as the notarial act.**

A notarial certificate must be executed at the same time (contemporaneously) as the notarial act.

----

29. Which of the following statements is **not** correct?

A. The principal signs and dates the notarial certificate.

B. A notarial certificate must state the jurisdiction where the notarial act is performed.

C. A notarial act is evidenced by a certificate and a stamp.

D. Certificates are executed at the same time as the notarial act.

29. **A. The principal signs and dates the notarial certificate**.

Choice "A" is not correct because the **NOTARY** signs and dates the notarial certificate.

----

30. An appeal from a decision regarding a notary commission goes to which court?

A. Town Appeals Court

B. County Appeals Court

C. City Court

D. none of the above

30. Answer: **D. none of the above**

An appeal from a decision regarding a notary commission goes to the **Appellate Division of the Superior Court**.

----

31. Which of the following two choices are correct? A person may be denied a notary public commission due to:

    1) conviction of a felony of the second degree or above

    2) conviction of any offense

A. 1 only is correct

B. 2 only is correct

C. Both 1 and 2 are correct.

D. Both 1 and 2 are not correct.

31. Answer: **A. 1 only is correct**

A person may be denied a notary public commission due to conviction of a felony of the second degree or above. (Minor offenses are not disqualifying.)

---

32. The _____ may deny a notary public commission if the applicant committed an incompetent or dishonest act which demonstrates that the applicant does not have the competence or reliability necessary to be a notary public.

A. County Clerk

B. State Controller

C. Attorney General

D. none of the above

32. Answer: **D. none of the above**

The **State Treasurer** may deny a notary public commission if the applicant committed an incompetent or dishonest act which demonstrates that the applicant does not have the competence or reliability necessary to be a notary public.

---

33. A notary who changes her name from the one she was commissioned shall notify the _____ and specify the circumstances of the name change.

A. State Treasurer

B. County Clerk

C. State Controller

D. none of the above

33. Answer: **A. State Treasurer**

A notary who changes her name from the one she was commissioned shall notify the **State Treasurer** and specify the circumstances of the name change.

---

34. The _____ must cancel and revoke a notary commission if oath is not taken within 3 months of receipt of the commission.

A. State Treasurer

B. State Controller

C. Attorney General

D. none of the above

34. Answer: **A. State Treasurer**

The **State Treasurer** must cancel and revoke a notary commission if oath is not taken within 3 months of receipt of the commission.

----

35. A resident or nonresident notary shall take an oath within _____ of receipt of original or renewal commission before which public officer.

A. 1 month

B. 2 months

C. 3 months

D. none of the above

35. Answer: **C. 3 months**

A resident or nonresident notary shall take an oath within **3 (THREE) months** of receipt of original or renewal commission before the county clerk.

----

36. What is the maximum fee that the State Treasurer can charge for each test administered online?

A. $10

B. $20

C. $25

D. none of the above

36. Answer: **D. none of the above**

The maximum fee that the State Treasurer can charge for each test administered online is **$15**.

----

37. The fee for the notary public application commission is:

A. $10

B. $20

C. $35

D. $25

37. Answer: **D. $25**

The fee for the notary public application commission is **$25**.

----

38. Choose the best answer. Which of the following applications must be sent electronically to the State Treasurer?

A. application for a notary public commission.

B. renewal application for a notary public commission.

C. both A and B.

D. neither A nor B.

38. Answer: **C. both A and B.**

BOTH an application for a notary public commission **AND** a renewal application for a notary public commission must be sent electronically to the **State Treasurer**.

----

39. Which of the following statements is correct? A notary public may advertise that he is an attorney:

A. if he is a law school enrollee.

B. if he has had some legal experience in New Jersey.

C. if he has worked as a legal assistant in a law firm.

D. none of the above

39. Answer: **D. none of the above**

A notary cannot advertise that he is an attorney unless he is in reality an attorney admitted to practice in New Jersey.

----

40. If a notary advertises in another language, he must include in the same advertisement a notice that:

    1) he is not an attorney

    2) he provides immigration legal advice.

A. 1 only

B. 2 only

C. both 1 and 2

D. neither 1 nor 2

40. Answer: **A. 1 only**

He must include in the same a notice that 1) he is not an attorney AND THAT 2) he **DOES NOT** provide immigration legal advice.

----

41. Which of the following notarial acts are voidable?

    1) a notarial act where the notary does not have a direct interest

    2) a notarial act where the spouse of the notary is a party

A. number 1 only

B. number 2 only

C. both 1 and 2

D. neither 1 nor 2

41. Answer: **B. number 2 only**

Choice 1) is <u>not</u> voidable. It would be voidable **IF** THE NOTARY DID HAVE A DIRECT INTEREST in the transaction.

----

42. A notary public commissioned in New Jersey may perform his duties:

A. in his state of birth and county of residence only.

B. only in the county where he is commissioned.

C. only in the county of birth and adjoining counties.

D. throughout the State of New Jersey.

42. Answer: **D. throughout the State of New Jersey.**

A notary public commissioned in New Jersey may perform his duties **throughout the State of New Jersey**.

----

43. Which of the following is **not** correct? To be commissioned a notary in New Jersey, a person may be the following:

A. a resident of New Jersey

B. employed in New Jersey

C. an attorney practicing in New Jersey

D. a legal secretary of the age of 17.

43. Answer: **D. a legal secretary of the age of 17.**

The minimum age to be commissioned a notary public is 18. The other three choices qualify to be a notary public.

----

44. The minimum age to be a notary public in the State of New Jersey is:

A. 16   **C. 18**

B. 17   D. 21

44. Answer: **C. 18**

The minimum age to be a notary public in the State of New Jersey is **18.**

----

45. Choose the best answer. To "sign" a document means which of the following?

A. to execute a tangible record

B. to associate with an electronic record an electronic symbol

C. to execute an oral contract

D. both A and B

45. Answer: **D. both A and B**

To "sign" a document means to execute a tangible record and to associate with an electronic record an electronic symbol.

----

46. Which of the following is the government officials who is empowered to commission notaries?

A. the Governor

B. the Commerce Commissioner

C. the State Treasurer

D. the Controller

46. Answer: **C. the State Treasurer**

The government officials who is empowered to commission notaries is the **State Treasurer**.

----

47. Which of the following is a notarial act?

A. acting as a guardian

B. taking a verification

C. acting as an executor of an estate

D. none of the above

47. Answer: **B. taking a verification**

A "notarial act" includes taking a verification, witnessing a signature, and administering an oath.

----

48. Acting as an authorized representative of another person is described as which of the following?

A. acting fraudulently

B. acting without established authority

C. acting in a representative capacity

D. none of the above

48. Answer: **C. acting in a representative capacity**

"In a representative capacity" means acting as an authorized representative of another in a capacity.

----

49. Choose the best answer. A document may be:

A. physical (tangible) or electronic

B. electronic.

C. physical (tangible)

D. None of the above choices are correct.

49. Answer: **A. physical (tangible) or electronic**

A document may be physical (tangible) or electronic.

----

50. "_____" is defined as a declaration made in front of a notary public that the person has signed a document, and if the person signed in a representative capacity, that the person had the authority to sign it.

A. affidavit

B. acknowledgment

C. compliance

D. contract

50. Answer: **B. acknowledgment**

"An **acknowledgment**" is defined as a declaration made in front of a notary public that the person has signed a document, and if the person signed in a representative capacity, that the person had the authority to sign it.

TEST 2 QUESTIONS

1.. In what location on the document page must the official stamp be affixed?

A. on a separate page of the document

B. at the beginning of the document

C. near the signature of the notary public.

D. on the first and last page of the document

2. The notary public official stamp must include which of the following?

A. the age of the notary

B. the title "Notary Public, State of New Jersey"

C. the nickname of the notary

D. the home address of the notary

3. Which of the following is correct?

A. A notarial certificate must state the date of birth of the notary.

B. A notarial certificate may be executed days after the notarial act.

C. A notarial certificate must state the date of issuance of the notary's commission.

D. A notary is required to sign the notarial certificate.

4. Which of the following statements is not correct?

A. A notarial act is evidenced solely by stamping a date on the document.

B. Certificates must be executed at the same time as the notarial act.

C. The notary signs and dates the notarial certificate.

D. A notarial certificate must state the jurisdiction where the notarial act is performed.

5. An appeal from a decision regarding a notary commission goes to which court?

A. Town Appeals Court

B. County Appeals Court

C. City Criminal Court

D. none of the above

6. Which of the following two choices are correct? A person may be denied a notary public commission due to:

    1) conviction of a petty offense

    2) failure to collect a notary fee

A. 1 only is correct

B. 2 only is correct

C. Both 1 and 2 are correct.

D. Both 1 and 2 are not correct.

7. The _____ may deny a notary public commission if the applicant committed an incompetent or dishonest act which demonstrates that the applicant does not have the competence or reliability necessary to be a notary public.

A. Governor

B. State Controller

C. State Treasurer

D. County Clerk

8. A notary who changes her name from the one she was commissioned shall notify the _____ and specify the circumstances of the name change.

A. County Clerk

B. State Controller

C. Attorney General

D. none of the above

9. The State Treasurer must cancel and revoke a notary commission if _____ within 3 months of receipt of the commission.

A. a copy of college diploma

B. a copy of high school diploma

C. $45 fee is not received

D. oath is not taken

10. Which of the following statements are correct? A _____ shall take an oath within 3 months of receipt of original or renewal commission before the county clerk.

A. a resident notary

B. a non-resident notary

C. Neither A nor B.

D. Both A and B.

11. What is the maximum fee that the State Treasurer can charge for each test administered online?

A. $5

B. $15

C. $25

D. $35

12. The fee for the notary public application commission is which of the following amounts?

A. $20   C. $35

B. $25   D. $30

13. An application or a renewal application for a notary public commission must be sent electronically to which of the following?

A. the State Controller

B. the State Treasurer

C. the Secretary of State

D. the County Clerk

14. Which of the following statements is correct? A notary public may advertise that he is an attorney:

A. if he has more than 3 years of legal experience in New Jersey.

B. If he is currently working as a legal assistant in a New Jersey law firm.

C. if he is studying commercial law in an accredited New Jersey college.

D. if he is an attorney admitted to the New Jersey bar.

15. If a notary advertises in another language, he must include in the same advertisement a notice that:

   1) he is an attorney

   2) he does not provide immigration legal advice.

A. 1 only   C. both 1 and 2

B. 2 only   D. neither 1 nor 2

16. Which of the following notarial acts are voidable?

   1) a notarial act where the notary has a direct interest

   2) a notarial act where a resident of the same town as the notary is a party

A. number 1 only

B. number 2 only

C. both 1 and 2

D. neither 1 nor 2

17. A notary public commissioned in New Jersey is authorized to perform his notarial duties:

A. only in his state of town or city of residence.

B. in every New Jersey county.

C. only in the county where he is commissioned.

D. in New Jersey and adjoining states.

18. Which of the following qualifies to be a notary in New Jersey?

A. a resident of Maryland who works in New York

B. 74 years-old retired teacher

C. a Pennsylvania attorney practicing in Virginia

D. 17 years-old college student working in a legal office in Trenton

19. Which of the following is not eligible to be commissioned a notary in New Jersey?

A. a male of the age of 72.

B. a female of the age of 19

C. a male of the age of 18

D. a male resident of New York who conducts all business in New York.

20. Which of the following has the same effect as signing a document?

A. to execute an oral contract

B. to associate with an electronic record an electronic symbol.

C. to agree by handshake

D. none of the above

21. Which New Jersey government officials is the official who commissions notaries public?

A. the Governor and the county clerks

B. the Commerce Commissioner

C. the State Attorney General

D. the State Treasurer

22. Choose the best answer. Which of the following is a notarial act?

A. administering an oath

B. taking a verification

C. both A and B

D. neither A nor B

23. Acting in a representative capacity means that the person is:

A. acting fraudulently

B. acting without established authority

C. acting is an attorney

D. an authorized representative of the person

24. Choose the best answer. A document presented to a notary may be:

A. physical (tangible)

B. physical (tangible) or electronic

C. electronic

D. intangible

25. An "acknowledgment" is defined as a declaration made in front of a _____ _____ that the person has signed a document, and if the person signed in a representative capacity, that the person had the authority to sign it.

A. secretary

B. clerk

C. city employee

D. notary public

26. The fee for administering oaths, taking affidavits, taking proofs of a deed, and taking acknowledgments of the grantors in the transfer of real estate, regardless of the number of such services performed in a single transaction to transfer real estate is:

A. $15.00

B. $20.00

C. $25.00

D. $35.00

27. For administering oaths, taking affidavits, taking proofs of a deed, and taking acknowledgements the fee is $_____ per act.

A. $2.00

B. $3.00

C. $10.00

D. none of the above

28. Which of the following choices is not correct? A notarial officer may refuse to perform a notarial act for a person that:

A. is not competent

B. did not sign the document

C. is over the age of 90

D. has a guardian appointed for him

29. Which of the following statements is correct? For remote notarization, the person:

A. must be located in an Indian territory

B. must be located in a New Jersey city

C. does not have to be located within the state of New Jersey

D. must be a person with disabilities

30. A notarial act that is done using remote technology for a person that is located in a remote location is considered done in New Jersey and is governed by _____ law.

A. federal

B. international

C. common

D. none of the above

31. A notary who intends on doing remote notarization must notify the _____ _____ before doing any remote notarization.

A. Secretary of State

B. State Controller

C. County Clerk

D. State Treasurer

32. Which of the following is not referred to as a "foreign state?"

A. Mexico

B. an Indian tribe

C. Canada

D. England

33. A "Digital Public key certificate" is which of the following?

A. photocopy code

B. photo ID

C. remote safe opener

D. none of the above

34. A systems that uses fingerprints, facial, and voice patterns to identify a person is referred to as a _____ identification system.

A. biometric

B. lithographic

C. photographic

D. none of the above

35. A government issued non-driver identification card is valid ID if not expired more than _____ before the notarial act.

A. one year

B. two years

C. three years

D. five years

36. Valid forms of satisfactory evidence of identity include which of the following?

A. college student card

B. a birth certificate

C. a U.S. passport

D. AARP Member Card

37. Which of the following choices is not correct?

A notary public may satisfy herself as to the identity of an individual by _____.

A. personal assurance of the individual

B. satisfactory evidence

C. personal knowledge

D. current government issued ID with photo

38. _____ who is a notary may instead of maintaining a notary journal, maintain a record of notarial acts in his office files.

A. a secretary and real estate broker

B. an attorney

C. a legal assistant

D. none of the above

39. Which fees must a notary record in the notary journal?

A. Fees greater than $10 in one sum only.

B. The sum of all fees.

C. Fees greater than $20 only (individually).

D. All fees individually

40. If the notary identified an individual by an identity document (ID) the notary must record in the notary journal the date of expiration and _____ of the identity document.

A. date of creation

B. the age of the person of the identity document

C. date of issuance

D. date of reissuance

41. If the notary knows an individual because of personal knowledge, what must the notary record in the notary journal?

A. that no notarization is required.

B. a statement to that effect.

C. the number of years of acquaintance.

D. none of the above

42. Choose the best answer. Which of the following two choices are correct? The notary journal must contain:

A. the name of each person for whom a notarial act was performed.

B. the amount of each fee collected by the notary.

C. Both are correct.

D. Both are not correct.

43. The fees charged for a notarial act:

A. do not have to be recorded in the notary journal if less than $15

B. must be recorded individually

C. may be recorded as one total sum

D. none of the above.

44. A notary must retain her notary journal for _____ year(s) after the notarial act.

A. 1

B. 5

C. 7

D. 10

45. If the notary journal is stolen or lost, the notary must notify the State Treasurer within _____ (at the State Treasurer's online site).

A. 72 hours

B. 3 days

C. 5 days

D. 10 days

46. Which of the following choices is not correct? The notary journal must contain:

A. the date and time of the notarial act

B. the type of notarial act

C. the name of each person for whom a notarial act was performed

D. the social security number of each person for whom a notarial act was performed

47. A notary journal maintained in a tangible medium must be:

  1) in a temporary medium

  2) in an unbound medium

A. 1 only

B. 2 only

C. both 1 and 2

D. neither 1 nor 2

48. Must a notary maintain separate notary journals for tangible and electronic notarizations?

A. Yes, if the entries are not sequentially numbered.

B. No. One notary journal must be kept.

C. Yes, only if the notary executes a document out of county.

D. Yes if the notary is commissioned after 2021.

49. If a notary stamping device is stolen, the notary must inform the State Treasurer within ____ calendar days.

A. 5

B. 15

C. 30

D. none of the above

50. Which of the following statements is not correct?

A. A notary is responsible for keeping a notary stamp secure.

B. Generally, a notary public can allow another person to use his stamp.

C. If an employer pays for a notary public device, the device does not become the property of the employer.

D. A notary stamp must include the title "Notary Public, State of New Jersey."

———————

TEST 2 ANSWER KEY

1.	C	11.	B	21.	D	31.	D	41.	B
2.	B	12.	B	22.	C	32.	B	42.	C
3.	D	13.	B	23.	D	33.	D	43.	B
4.	A	14.	D	24.	B	34.	A	44.	D
5.	D	15.	B	25.	D	35.	C	45.	D
6.	D	16.	A	26.	A	36.	C	46.	D
7.	C	17.	B	27.	D	37.	A	47.	D
8.	D	18.	B	28.	C	38.	B	48.	B
9.	D	19.	D	29.	C	39.	D	49.	D
10.	D	20.	B	30.	D	40.	C	50.	B

TEST 2 ANSWERS

1. In what location on the document page must the official stamp be affixed?

A. on a separate page of the document

B. at the beginning of the document

C. near the signature of the notary public.

D. on the first and last page of the document

1. Answer: **C. near the signature of the notary public.**

The official stamp must be affixed near the signature of the notary public.

----

2. The notary public official stamp must include which of the following?

A. the age of the notary

B. the title "Notary Public, State of New Jersey"

C. the nickname of the notary

D. the home address of the notary

2. Answer: **B. the title "Notary Public, State of New Jersey"**

The notary public official stamp must include the title "Notary Public, State of New Jersey."

----

3. Which of the following is correct?

A. A notarial certificate must state the date of birth of the notary.

B. A notarial certificate may be executed days after the notarial act.

C. A notarial certificate must state the date of issuance of the notary's commission.

D. A notary is required to sign the notarial certificate.

3. Answer: **D. A notary is required to sign the notarial certificate.**

A notary is required to date and sign a notarial certificate which the notary issues.

----

4. Which of the following statements is **not** correct?

A. A notarial act is evidenced solely by stamping a date on the document.

B. Certificates must be executed at the same time as the notarial act.

C. The notary signs and dates the notarial certificate.

D. A notarial certificate must state the jurisdiction where the notarial act is performed.

4. Answer: **A. A notarial act is evidenced solely by stamping a date on the document**.

Choice "A" is **not** correct because a notarial act is evidenced by **a certificate and a stamp**.

----

5. An appeal from a decision regarding a notary commission goes to which court?

A. Town Appeals Court

B. County Appeals Court

C. City Criminal Court

D. none of the above

5. Answer: **D. none of the above**

An appeal from a decision regarding a notary commission goes to the **Appellate Division of the Superior Court**

----

6. Which of the following two choices are correct? A person may be denied a notary public commission due to:

    1) conviction of a petty offense

    2) failure to collect a notary fee.

A. 1 only is correct

B. 2 only is correct

C. Both 1 and 2 are correct.

D. Both 1 and 2 are not correct.

6. Answer: **D. Both 1 and 2 are not correct.**

A person may be denied a notary public commission due to conviction of a crime of the second degree or above. (Minor offenses are not disqualifying.) A notary may waive charging a fee.

----

7. The _____ may deny a notary public commission if the applicant committed an incompetent or dishonest act which demonstrates that the applicant does not have the competence or reliability necessary to be a notary public.

A. Governor

B. State Controller

C. State Treasurer

D. County Clerk

7. Answer: **C. State Treasurer**

The **State Treasurer** may deny a notary public commission if the applicant committed an incompetent or dishonest act which demonstrates that the applicant does not have the competence or reliability necessary to be a notary public.

----

8. A notary who changes her name from the one she was commissioned shall notify the _____ and specify the circumstances of the name change.

A. County Clerk

B. State Controller

C. Attorney General

D. none of the above

8. Answer: **D. none of the above**

A notary who changes her name from the one she was commissioned shall notify the **State Treasurer** and specify the circumstances of the name change.

----

9. The State Treasurer must cancel and revoke a notary commission if _____ within 3 months of receipt of the commission.

A. a copy of college diploma

B. a copy of high school diploma

C. $45 fee is not received

D. oath is not taken

9. Answer: **D. oath is not taken**

The State Treasurer must cancel and revoke a notary commission if **oath is not taken** within 3 months of receipt of the commission.

----

10. Choose the best answer. Which of the following statements is correct? A _____ shall take an oath within 3 months of receipt of original or renewal commission before the county clerk.

A. a resident notary

B. a non-resident notary

C. Neither A nor B.

D. Both A and B.

10. Answer: **D. Both A and B.**

A **resident and nonresident notary** shall take an oath within 3 months of receipt of original or renewal commission before which public officer.

----

11. What is the maximum fee that the State Treasurer can charge for each test administered online?

A. $5   C. $25

B. $15   D. $35

11. Answer: **B. $15**

The maximum fee that the State Treasurer can charge for each test administered online is **$15**.

----

12. The fee for the notary public application commission is which of the following amounts?

A. $20

B. $25

C. $35

D. $30

12. Answer: **B. $25**

The fee for the notary public application commission is **$25**.

----

13. An application or a renewal application for a notary public commission must be sent electronically to which of the following?

A. the State Controller

B. the State Treasurer

C. the Secretary of State

D. the County Clerk

13. Answer: **B. the State Treasurer**

An application or a renewal application for a notary public commission must be sent electronically to **the State Treasurer**.

----

14. Which of the following statements is correct? A notary public may advertise that he is an attorney:

A. if he has more than 3 years of legal experience in New Jersey.

B. If he is currently working as a legal assistant in a New Jersey law firm.

C. if he is studying commercial law in an accredited New Jersey college.

D. if he is an attorney admitted to the New Jersey bar.

14. Answer: **D. if he is an attorney admitted to the New Jersey bar.**

A notary public may advertise that he is an attorney **ONLY IF** he is actually an attorney admitted to the New Jersey bar.

----

15. If a notary advertises in another language, he must include in the same a notice that:

1) he is an attorney

2) he does not provide immigration legal advice.

A. 1 only

B. 2 only

C. both 1 and 2

D. neither 1 nor 2

15. Answer: **B. 2 only**

He must include in the same a notice that 1) he is **NOT** an attorney and that 2) he does not provide immigration legal advice.

----

16. Which of the following notarial acts are voidable?

   1) a notarial act where the notary has a direct interest

   2) a notarial act where a resident of the same town as the notary is a party

A. number 1 only

B. number 2 only

C. both 1 and 2

D. neither 1 nor 2

16. Answer: **A. number 1 only**

Choice 1) is voidable because notaries are prohibited from notarizing documents when they have a direct interest in the transaction. The fact that a person resides in the same town is not a disqualifying factor.

----

17. A notary public commissioned in New Jersey is authorized to perform his notarial duties:

A. only in his state of town or city of residence.

B. in every New Jersey county.

C. only in the county where he is commissioned.

D. in New Jersey and adjoining states.

17. Answer: **B. in every New Jersey county.**

A notary public commissioned in New Jersey may perform his duties **throughout the State of New Jersey.**

----

18. Which of the following qualifies to be a notary in New Jersey?

A. a resident of Maryland who works in New York

B. 74 years-old retired teacher

C. a Pennsylvania attorney practicing in Virginia

D. 17 years-old college student working in a legal office in Trenton

18. Answer: **B. 74 years-old retired teacher**

This is the answer because there is no upper limit for age to be commissioned a notary public.

----

19. Which of the following is **not** eligible to be commissioned a notary in New Jersey?

A. a male of the age of 72.

B. a female of the age of 19

C. a male of the age of 18

D. a male resident of New York who conducts all business in New York.

19. Answer: **D. a male resident of New York who conducts all business in New York.**

To be commissioned a notary in New Jersey, a person may be 1) a resident on New Jersey, OR 2) employed in New Jersey, OR 3) an attorney practicing in New Jersey.

----

20. Which of the following has the same effect as signing a document?

A. to execute an oral contract

B. to associate with an electronic record an electronic symbol.

C. to agree by handshake

D. none of the above

20. Answer: **B. to associate with an electronic record an electronic symbol.**

To "sign" means to execute a tangible record, or to associate with an electronic record an electronic symbol.

----

21. Which New Jersey government officials is the official who commissions notaries public?

A. the Governor and the county clerks

B. the Commerce Commissioner

C. the State Attorney General

D. the State Treasurer

21. Answer: **D. the State Treasurer**

The government officials who is empowered to commission notaries is the State Treasurer.

----

22. Chose the best answer. Which of the following is a notarial act?

A. administering an oath

B. taking a verification

C. both A and B

D. neither A nor B

22. Answer: **C. both A and B**

A "notarial act" includes taking a verification, witnessing a signature, and administering an oath.

----

23. Acting in a representative capacity means that the person is:

A. acting fraudulently

B. acting without established authority

C. acting is an attorney

D. an authorized representative of the person

23. Answer: **D. an authorized representative of the person.**

Acting in a representative capacity means that the person is an authorized representative of the person.

----

24. Choose the best answer. A document presented to a notary may be:

A. physical (tangible)

B. physical (tangible) or electronic

C. electronic

D. intangible

24. Answer: **B. physical (tangible) or electronic**

A document presented to a notary may be physical (tangible) or electronic.

----

25. An "acknowledgment" is defined as a declaration made in front of a _____ _____ that the person has signed a document, and if the person signed in a representative capacity, that the person had the authority to sign it.

A. secretary

B. clerk

C. city employee

D. notary public

25. **Answer: D. notary public**

"An acknowledgment" is defined as a declaration made in front of a **notary public** that the person has signed a document, and if the person signed in a representative capacity, that the person had the authority to sign it.

----

26. The fee for administering oaths, taking affidavits, taking proofs of a deed, and taking acknowledgments of the grantors in the transfer of real estate, regardless of the number of such services performed in a single transaction to transfer real estate is:

A. $15.00

B. $20.00

C. $25.00

D. $35.00

26. Answer: **A. $15.00**

Fee for administering oaths, taking affidavits, taking proofs of a deed, and taking acknowledgments of the grantors in the transfer of real estate, regardless of the number of such services performed in a single transaction to **transfer real estate** is **$15.00**.

NOTE ALSO that the fee for administering oaths, taking affidavits, and taking acknowledgments of the mortgagors in the financing of real estate, regardless of the number of such services performed in a single transaction to **finance real estate** is **$25.00**.

----

27. For administering oaths, taking affidavits, taking proofs of a deed, and taking acknowledgements the fee is $_____ per act.

A. $2.00

B. $3.00

C. $10.00

D. none of the above

27. Answer: **D. none of the above**

For administering oaths, taking affidavits, taking proofs of a deed, and taking acknowledgements the fee is **$2.50** per act.

----

28. Which of the following choices is **not** correct? A notarial officer may refuse to perform a notarial act for a person that:

A. is not competent

B. did not sign the document

C. is over the age of 90

D. has a guardian appointed for him

28. Answer: **C. is over the age of 90**

A notarial officer may **NOT** refuse to perform a notarial act solely for the reason that a person is over the age of 90.

----

29. Which of the following statements is correct? For remote notarization, the person:

A. must be located in an Indian territory

B. must be located in a New Jersey city

C. does not have to be located within the state of New Jersey

D. must be a person with disabilities

29. Answer: **C. does <u>NOT</u> have to be located within the state of New Jersey.**

For remote notarization, the person does <u>NOT</u> have to be located within the state of New Jersey.

----

30. A notarial act that is done using remote technology for a person that is located in a remote location is considered done in New Jersey and is governed by _____ law.

A. federal

B. international

C. common

D. none of the above

30. Answer: **D. none of the above**

A notarial act that is done using remote technology for a person that is located in a remote location is considered done in New Jersey and is governed by **New Jersey** law.

----

31. A notary who intends on doing remote notarization must notify the _____ _____ before doing any remote notarization.

A. Secretary of State

B. State Controller

C. County Clerk

D. State Treasurer

31. Answer: **D. State Treasurer**

A notary who intends on doing remote notarization must notify the **State Treasurer** before doing any remote notarization.

32. Which of the following is **<u>not</u>** referred to as a "foreign state?"

A. Mexico

B. an Indian tribe

C. Canada

D. England

32. Answer: **B. an Indian tribe**

A political entity (**other** than a U.S. state, an Indian tribe, or the United States) is known as a "**foreign**" state.

----

33. A "Digital Public key certificate" is which of the following?

A. photocopy code

B. photo ID

C. remote safe opener

D. none of the above

33. Answer: **D. none of the above**

A "Digital Public Key Certificate" is an **electronic credential**.

----

34. A systems that uses fingerprints, facial, and voice patterns to identify a person is referred to as a _____ identification system.

A. biometric

B. lithographic

C. photographic

D. none of the above

34. Answer: **A biometric**

A systems that uses fingerprints, facial, and voice patterns to identify a person is referred to as a **biometric** identification system.

----

35. A government issued non-driver identification card is valid ID if not expired more than _____ before the notarial act.

A. one year

B. two years

C. three years

D. five years

35. Answer: **C. 3 years**

A government issued non-driver identification card is valid ID if not expired more than **3 (THREE) years** before the notarial act.

----

36. Valid forms of satisfactory evidence of identity include which of the following?

A. college student card

B. a birth certificate

C. a U.S. passport

D. AARP Member Card

36. Answer: **C. a U.S. passport**

Valid forms of satisfactory evidence of identity include a **passport, driver's license, or government-issued, non- driver ID card**.

----

37. Which of the following choices is **not** correct?

A notary public may satisfy herself as to the identity of an individual by _____.

A. personal assurance of the individual

B. satisfactory evidence

C. personal knowledge

D. current government issued ID with photo

37. Answer: **A. personal assurance by the individual**

A notary public may satisfy herself as to the identity of an individual by satisfactory evidence, and personal knowledge, and current government issued ID with photo.

Personal assurance of the individual is **not** acceptable.

----

38. _____ who is a notary may instead of maintaining a notary journal maintain a record of notarial acts in his office files.

A. a secretary and real estate broker

B. an attorney

C. a legal assistant

D. none of the above

38. Answer: **B. an attorney**

An attorney who is a notary may instead of maintaining a notary journal, maintain a record of notarial acts in his office files.

----

39. Which fees must a notary record in the notary journal?

A. Fees greater than $10 in one sum only.

B. The sum of all fees.

C. Fees greater than $20 only (individually).

D. All fees individually

39. Answer: **D. All fees individually**

A notary must record **individually all fees** in the notary journal.

----

40. If the notary identified an individual by an identity document (ID) the notary must record in the notary journal the date of expiration and _____ of the identity document.

A. date of creation

B. the age of the person of the identity document

C. date of issuance

D. date of reissuance

40. Answer: **C. date of issuance**

If the notary identified an individual by an identity document (ID) the notary must record in the notary journal the **date of issuance and date of expiration** of the identity document.

----

41. If the notary knows an individual because of personal knowledge, what must the notary record in the notary journal?

A. that no notarization is required.

B. a statement to that effect.

C. the number of years of acquaintance.

D. none of the above

41. Answer: **B. a statement to that effect.**

If the notary knows an individual because of personal knowledge, the notary must record in the notary journal **a statement to that effect.**

----

42. Which of the following two choices are correct? The notary journal must contain:

A. the name of each person for whom a notarial act was performed.

B. the amount of each fee collected by the notary.

C. Both are correct.

D. Both are not correct.

42. Answer: **C. Both are correct.**

The notary journal must contain the name of each person for whom a notarial act was performed, and the amount of each fee collected by the notary.

----

43. The fees charged for a notarial act:

A. do not have to be recorded in the notary journal if less than $15

B. must be recorded individually

C. may be recorded as one total sum

D. none of the above

43. Answer: **B. must be recorded individually**.

The fees charged for a notarial act must be recorded individually.

----

44. A notary must retain her notary journal for _____ year(s) after the notarial act.

A. 1   C. 7

B. 5   **D. 10**

44. Answer: **D. 10**

A notary must retain her notary journal for **10 (TEN) years** after the notarial act.

----

45. If the notary journal is stolen or lost, the notary must notify the State Treasurer within _____ (at the State Treasurer's online site).

A. 72 hours   C. 5 days

B. 3 days   **D. 10 days**

45. Answer: **D. 10 days**

If the notary journal is stolen or lost, the notary must notify the State Treasurer within **10 DAYS** (at the State Treasurer's online site).

----

46. Which of the following choices is not correct? The notary journal must contain:

A. the date and time of the notarial act

B. the type of notarial act

C. the name of each person for whom a notarial act was performed

D. the social security number of each person for whom a notarial act was performed

46. Answer: **D. the social security number of each person for whom a notarial act was performed**

Choice "D" is not correct because social security numbers are never required.

----

47. A notary journal maintained in a tangible medium must be:

 1) in a temporary medium

 2) in an unbound medium

A. 1 only

B. 2 only

C. both 1 and 2

D. neither 1 nor 2

47. Answer: **D. neither 1 nor 2**

A notary journal maintained in a tangible medium must be **1) in a <u>permanent</u> medium AND 2) bound medium.**

----

48. Must a notary maintain separate notary journals for tangible and electronic notarizations?

A. Yes, if the entries are not sequentially numbered.

B. No. One notary journal must be kept.

C. Yes, only if the notary executes a document out of county.

D. Yes if the notary is commissioned after 2021.

48. Answer: **B. No. One notary journal must be kept.**

In all cases, **ONE** notary journal for both tangible and electronic notarizations must be kept.

----

49. If a notary stamping device is stolen, the notary must inform the State Treasurer within ____ calendar days.

A. 5

B. 15

C. 30

D. none of the above

49. Answer: **D. none of the above**

If a notary stamping device is stolen, the notary must inform the State Treasurer within **10 (TEN) calendar days**.

----

50. Which of the following statements is **not** correct?

A. A notary is responsible for keeping a notary stamp secure.

B. Generally, a notary public can allow another person to use his stamp.

C. If an employer pays for a notary public device, the device does not become the property of the employer.

D. A notary stamp must include the title "Notary Public, State of New Jersey."

50. Answer: **B. Generally, a notary public can allow another person to use his stamp.**

Choice "B" is **not** correct because generally, a notary public **cannot** allow another person to use his stamp.

New Jersey requires that notaries public maintain one combined NOTARY JOURNAL for traditional and electronic notarial acts. We have prepared an inexpensive NOTARY JOURNAL specifically for New Jersey. It is:

"New Jersey Notary Journal for Traditional and Electronic Notarial Acts"

(2 entries on a page)

1	☐ Acknowledgment ☐ Oath/Affirmation ☐ Proof of a Deed	Date and Time of Notarial Act
Fee:_____ _____ _____		_____

Signer Name (print)	Witness Name (print)	
Phone #I	Phone #I	___ Tangible Record ___ Electronic Record
Address	Address	**Itemized Fees**
ID Type: ___Driver License ___ Passport ___Personal Knowledge ___ ID Card ___Credible Witness ___ See Notes	ID Type: ___Driver License ___Passport ___Personal Knowledge ___ID Card ___Credible Witness ___ See Notes	**Other Notes**
ID. Issued by	ID. Issued by	
Expiration Date	Expiration Date	
I.D. Number	I.D. Number	
Issue Date	Issue Date	
Signer Signature	Witness Signature	

_____

Credits
Cover image: David Merret. Flickr.com. 2.0 Generic (CC BY 2.0)
Quote on cover: Wikipedia.org